P9-EEA-008

MOTIVATING YOUR KIDS
FROM CRAYONS TO CAREER

. . . is a timely book packed with:

* Helpful methods for challenging and supporting
  your kids for success at school and throughout their
  lives
* Easy-to-apply learning ideas and practical suggestions supported by specific examples
* Insights into how and why children are motivated
  or demotivated

Is your child learning at school or simply making the
grade? Kids need to be motivated to *learn* in school to
achieve true success. Now, with this innovative new book,
you can open your child's eyes to the joys of learning and
the benefits of knowledge.

Most Berkley Books are available at special quantity discounts for bulk purchases for sales promotions, premiums, fund raising, or educational use. Special books or book excerpts can also be created to fit specific needs.

For details, write or telephone Special Markets, The Berkley Publishing Group, 200 Madison Avenue, New York, New York 10016; (212) 951-8800.

MOTIVATING YOUR KIDS FROM Crayons TO CAREER

HOW TO ENHANCE YOUR CHILD'S LEARNING AND ACHIEVEMENT—WITHOUT PRESSURE!

by

CHERI FULLER

BERKLEY BOOKS, NEW YORK

Scripture quotations marked NAS are taken from the *New American Standard Bible.* Copyright © The Lockman Foundation 1960, 1962, 1963, 1968, 1971, 1972, 1973, 1975, 1977.

Verses marked TLB are taken from *The Living Bible* © 1971. Used by permission of Tyndale House Publishers, Inc., Wheaton, IL 60189. All rights reserved.

Some Scripture is from the *Good News Bible, Today's English Version,* Copyright © American Bible Society, 1966, 1971, 1976. Used by permission.

This Berkley book contains the complete
text of the original edition.

MOTIVATING YOUR KIDS FROM CRAYONS TO CAREER

A Berkley Book / published by arrangement with
Honor Books, a division of Harrison House, Inc.

PRINTING HISTORY
Honor Books edition published 1990
Berkley edition / September 1991

All rights reserved.
Copyright © 1990 by Cheri Fuller.
This book may not be reproduced in whole or in part,
by mimeograph or any other means, without permission.
For information address: Honor Books, a division of Harrison House, Inc.,
P.O. Box 55388, Tulsa, Oklahoma 74155-1388.

ISBN: 0-425-12907-1

A BERKLEY BOOK ® TM 757,375
Berkley Books are published by The Berkley Publishing Group,
200 Madison Avenue, New York, New York 10016.
The name "BERKLEY" and the "B" logo
are trademarks belonging to Berkley Publishing Corporation.

PRINTED IN THE UNITED STATES OF AMERICA

10 9 8 7 6 5 4 3 2 1

CONTENTS

ACKNOWLEDGMENTS

I want to express my thanks to my husband, Holmes, for his love, faithfulness, and support during our twenty years of marriage and throughout the writing of this book; and to Justin, Chris, and Alison for their confidence in me and their encouraging words of "Mom, you can do it!" in the midst of difficult, hectic times and deadlines.

For suggestions and contributions I am grateful to Melanie Hemry, Lynn Fuller, Joanna Smith, Gordon Corbett, Dr. Carol Kelly, Dr. David Elkind, Dr. Arthur Bodin, Dr. Jeff Smith, Mrs. Edith Schaeffer, Karen Gale, Kay Bishop, Connie Baker, Marilyn Phillips and Debbie Leslie. For the work of Dorothy Corkille Briggs, for the research and writing of Dr. Priscilla Vail, Dr. Howard Gardner, and Louise Bates Ames I am grateful. Thank you to Flo Perkins for prayer and caring. A special thank you to my sisters, Marilyn Morgan and Georgia Linam, and my brother, George Heath, for their love and encouragement. And many thanks to all the parents, teachers, and children who shared their experiences and ideas!

I greatly appreciate my publishers, Buddy Harrison and Keith Provance, and my editor, Cris Bolley, for their enthusiasm and support of this project. Thanks to Linda Overton and Karen Dee for their kindness and help; to

Jimmy Peacock and Michal Taylor for their editorial work; to Nancy Titolo for her creative design; and to the whole staff of Honor Books.

Most of all, I am thankful that the love of the Father we sang of as children in "Jesus loves me this I know, for the Bible tells me so" is just as true and alive today, and has sustained and encouraged me in the writing of this book and throughout my life. For us as parents and our children, God can provide the ultimate motivation to live and love, to grow and become all we are meant to be.

This book is dedicated to
all children
who dream
about the future

8

SOMEDAY

One of the biggest concerns I hear expressed in the parents' groups and in numerous PTA and magazine surveys conducted across the country, is "How do we motivate our children for learning and school achievement?" As parents, we all want our children to be the best students they can be. We have high hopes for them. But despite our best intentions, many of today's kids are unmotivated. And many of us are pushing our kids too far too fast and they are becoming burned out by the stress they face everyday both in and out of school.

As I have been with elementary-aged children for the past several months teaching creative writing, I have been struck as I have listened to them express their own "great expectations" for the future. Just recently I sat in a circle with twenty-five precious, energetic seven- and eight-year-olds. It was a very important day! After working on their writing for weeks, each child had an opportunity to sit in the "author's chair" and read his "SOMEDAY" book.

Bright, original images of butterflies, balloons, horses, jets, and helicopters decorated the covers of their work. Hardbound, handwritten, and illustrated, each book expressed the child's hopes and dreams for the future. As Cary, our first author, read, "This book is dedicated to Mom and Dad," her wiggly classmates grew very attentive.

Some were interested in gaining fame and fortune as movie stars; others sought adventure and travel, hoping to go around the world and learn other languages. Some desired a career in sports, wanting to be a great basketball player like Michael Jordan, or win a gold medal in the Olympics. Some of their dreams were fanciful — wanting to take a ride in a hot-air balloon, see it snow on the Fourth of July, or invent a roller coaster that would go faster than the speed of light.

And many of the children's hopes were serious: "Someday I will stop all drugs!" or, "Someday I will make lots of money and pay all my Grandma's bills" or, "Someday I will help the homeless." Their books also reflected their interests in careers and their goals for what they would like to be when they grow up:

"Someday I'm going to be a biologist and study snakes."

"Someday I'm going to be a doctor and find a cure for cancer."

"Someday I'm going to be a writer and publish children's books."

"Someday I'm going to be an astronaut and explore Venus and Mars."

Architects, nurses, teachers, scientists — and "Someday I'm going to be just like my dad!"

Children *are* our nation's future, and as I sat there with them, inspired by their hopes and plans for the days to come, I thought, how can we as parents and teachers help kids get the foundation and education they will need to stay motivated and meet the challenges which lie ahead to realize all of their wonderful plans and dreams?

Chapter 1

MOTIVATION:
WHAT IS IT?

Recently I watched a national television program whose theme was the motivation of children for school achievement. First, four young boys sitting on a stage were interviewed.

"Why didn't you make better grades?" they were asked.

"I dunno," answered the sixth grader.

"Why didn't you do your home work?" queried the interviewer. "Don't you know how important an education is?"

Their answers were similarly vague — until they were asked, "What's your favorite subject?"

"Lunch!" they quickly responded. "P.E.!"

Then I cringed, and so did the five school-aged youngsters watching with me, as the report cards of two of the boys, revealing failing grades, were flashed on the television screen for all the nation to see. The youngsters' faces fell, their humiliation complete.

Then the boys' frustrated mothers were interviewed.

"What did you do to try to motivate your son to do better?" they were each asked.

"Well, I grounded him, took away his bike and after-school time, and made him sit and do his homework," the first mother responded. "But his grades didn't get any better."

"What did you do to try to get your son to make better grades?" the second mother was asked.

"I nagged," she replied. "I threatened bodily harm and I carried out my threats. I took away his dessert."

"I talked to his teacher and told her to get tough," another mother added. "I took away his Nintendo."

Then a special guest, an educational consultant, came on to offer the distraught mothers some expert advice.

"Have a study desk, materials, and quiet during study time," he counseled. "Make your children do their homework, even if they have to sit there all evening."

"But I've done that," mother number two protested. "It never worked."

Although the intentions of those who produced and participated in that program were good, I wondered why they had not stressed all the positive ways children can be motivated for learning and achievement — *without* threats, *without* pressure and *without* bodily harm!

Why are so many of the methods used in homes and schools to "motivate" children actually negative responses that stifle motivation, destroy self-esteem and produce —

or increase — an intense hatred for school, study and homework?

Motivation Defined

What is *motivation* anyway?

Webster defines it as "an inner drive that causes one to act; [an] incentive." To motivate also means to "inspire hope, stimulate, propel, spur, whet, fire, and trigger."[1]

When we talk about a "motivated learner," we are referring to the young person who has caught a feeling of excitement about learning a skill, who is enthusiastic about the task at hand — whether at home or at school. It is the self-starter, the student who takes the initiative to jot down ideas and assignments without being asked. He* begins the science project long before the last night! If he hits an obstacle and fails to grasp a concept, he seeks help. He doesn't give up just because a challenge is difficult, but has the inner fire to keep going in spite of setbacks, to keep plugging away until "the light comes on."

The question is: how can we motivate our children for learning without pressuring them? How can we whet an appetite for knowledge, the desire to know and understand more about the world around them? How can we trigger in them an excitement about discovery and science? How can we set off the spark within them that will propel them to keep trying to learn and grow in spite of obstacles and challenges?

Children are naturally curious. They come into the world motivated — eager to learn, touch, explore, question, discover. How do we fan the flame of that innate motivation rather than extinguish it?

---

* The information in this book applies to both boys and girls. "He" is used in odd numbered chapters and "she" is used in even numbered chapters.

Also, some names have been changed to protect privacy.

As parents, we can help with activities and attitudes that generate a child's enthusiasm for learning. Each child has a different and unique personality. Some are go-getters — some naturally slow, cautious starters. Some seem to be born with an inner drive to get things done. Some are easygoing or late bloomers. Although we can't *make* the fire catch, we can rub two sticks together, pour some starter fluid on, and fan the flame. There are many ways we can help children get started, build up steam, and go the distance in this "marathon" of learning and education.

Boosting Children's Motivation

In this book I will offer concrete ways to *boost children's motivation:* a close, loving parent-child relationship; avoidance of the pitfalls of pressure, stress, burnout, and perfectionism; the maintenance of a healthy perspective on grades; the power of positive, but realistic expectations, of patience, and of positive role-modeling. I will also share specific "motivation boosters," such as building on a child's natural strengths, learning style, and interests; developing his language skills; storytelling; encouraging a lively curiosity; awakening the latent power of observation; and creating cultural and geographical awareness.

We will discuss some "motivation busters" and how to overcome them: a lack of attention skills, absence due to sickness, and school transfers.

Finally, we will look at how single-parent families can provide a solid background for motivating children for learning and achievement.

Motivation, the precious spark within each child, can be nurtured at home and reinforced at school. So let's look at all the ways we can kindle, not dampen, the fires of enthusiasm and motivation in our children, creating in them a love of learning and the positive, "can-do" attitudes they will need to achieve in the classroom and in the world.

Chapter 2

THE FOUNDATION: BUILDING A CLOSE PARENT-CHILD RELATIONSHIP

Why include a chapter on building the parent-child relationship in a book about motivating children for learning? Because we know that motivated children tend to be those who have a close, loving relationship with their parents.

If the parent-child relationship is weak, all the enriching academic programs and school reforms will not result in motivated kids who are interested in learning. For we know that unmet emotional needs block learning in children. The child starved for love, acceptance, and attention from her parents has scant energy to face the challenges of school.

Studies of the most motivated students in a California high school showed that those who were doing well, those who had high goals and achievement records, were the ones whose parents stayed involved with them in their early years and throughout their high school career. The parents of successful students were "engaged" with their children. They talked about interesting things the youngsters were doing. They resisted the temptation to provide their children with a lot of early freedom in dating and driving. They were not inordinately harsh or over-protective, but established clear boundaries of behavior. They showed a real interest in their children's lives in school and out. *They made parenting a priority, spending a great deal of time with their children.* [1]

A secure parent-child relationship is a major foundation for a child's self-esteem. And the young person with high self-esteem is more motivated for learning and for life. With a positive view of herself, a youngster can set high goals, take risks needed for learning and achievement, and keep working toward those goals even in the face of obstacles and setbacks.

As Dorothy Corkille Briggs notes: "Your child's judgment of himself influences the kinds of friends he chooses, how he gets along with others, the kind of person he marries, and how productive he will be. It affects his creativity, integrity, stability, and even whether he will be a leader or a follower. His feelings of self-worth form the core of his aptitudes and abilities. His attitude toward himself has a direct bearing on how he lives all parts of his life. In fact, *self-esteem is the mainspring that slates every child for success or failure as a human being.*"[2]

Our children may bump up against people outside the family who give them negative feedback, or they may go through hurtful or difficult experiences, but their time spent at home, especially the early years, will set the stage for whether they will establish and maintain healthy, positive patterns of behavior, or negative, destructive ones.

And one of the ways we can foster high self-esteem, a feeling of being loved and worthwhile (not conceit or a bragging, superior attitude, which is merely a cover-up for insecurity and a sense of low self-worth) is to establish a strong parent-child relationship between us and our offspring.

What's It All About?

One day after I had dropped off my daughter Alison at a babysitting job and had taken my son, Chris, and his friend to play basketball, I was on my way home to thaw out some hamburgers to cook for dinner. Suddenly this thought occurred to me:

What is parenting all about?

I reflected on the joy of giving birth to a precious baby and the nights spent walking her when she is colicky. It's spring stroller rides and teething times, toilet training, and the first day of school.

Parenting is about all the responsibility of teaching and training, providing, loving, and caring. It includes taking the child to the doctor or dentist, giving her birthday parties, dropping her off at piano lessons, and coming back to pick her up again forty-five minutes later. It's fixing a lunch box and sending it along with her to school. It's helping her with her homework. It's running her from here to there at all hours of the day and night, from scouts to baseball practice to church activities.

But parenting is more than that.

With little ones, it is diapering bottoms and wiping noses and reading "Pat the Bunny" for the "umpteenth time."

But parenting is more than that.

As children grow, it includes operating a taxi service, a laundry service, an educational consulting service, and a counseling service. It is grabbing a smorgasbord dinner off the counter "in shifts" before open house or school carnival night. It is nursing them through the flu and mononucleosis. Later, it is staying up and waiting for them to come home from the senior prom.

But parenting is more than this, I thought. *It's also about building a relationship with a child that will last a lifetime.*

In the final analysis, parenting is about learning how to listen and how to communicate. It is learning how to love unconditionally this changing, growing person who is so like us and yet so completely different from us. It is learning to let go, realizing and accepting that as she grows, she will develop independence and will eventually stand on her own two feet.

As a professor once said, the key ingredient in the successful development of a human being is the fact that some adult is crazy about her — crazy enough to put her and her welfare before career, ambitions, the acquisition of things, or a new spouse. Someone is crazy enough about her to take time to build bridges, to form a strong relationship with her.

That someone is the parent.

Building Bridges

> "It is hard to develop *any* self-worth without a close personal link to at least one adult."
>
> Eve Bither
> Maine Commissioner of Education

Building a relationship with a child is not always an easy task. In the early years it is not unusual for us to get busy and miss opportunities for bridge-building. When children are little, we're often trying to get (and keep!) them occupied; getting them busy with an activity; taking them to be with friends or relatives, to the babysitter, or to school; so we can cook, clean house, and do our important adult tasks which we feel so time-pressed about.

And it doesn't get any easier as the child moves into the middle years from elementary school to junior high and high school. As she progresses, her schedule becomes so filled that she has difficulty working *us* in! (My, how the tables turn!)

Often what's missing in the parent-child relationship is a *bridge,* some common ground both parent and child can relate to, something they can both enjoy doing together.

A bridge is something that provides a connection or contact, something that spans or links. In the parent-child relationship, a bridge is built brick by brick, moment by moment, during the time the two spend together with each other. And the thing that helps — a key to building the parent-child relationship — is finding something that both parent and child are interested in, enjoy doing, and can share together.

"It's important to be doing something *together*, not just something *for* the child, but something you really enjoy; not just as a reward or a duty, but as having found out and discovered something that can be talked about and shared when you're together," says Edith Schaeffer, mother, grandmother and great-grandmother, and author of *What Is a Family?*[3]

Discovering and doing something you and your child both enjoy builds a relationship.

Bridge-building is not just doing something *for* the child in a patronizing way, not just spending time with her because the book says to. Rather, it is sharing together an enjoyable moment, a pleasurable activity, because both want to, for their own sakes, as well as for the sake of the other.

As a parent, I want to *know* my children: Chris, Justin and Alison. Life is so short, and I don't want their growing years to slip by (as they so quickly do). I don't want to wake up one day, after they have grown up and left, and wish we had been closer or that we had spent more time together. Any parent's life is diminished when he and his children do not have a close relationship. Knowing and relating to my children helps me grow, and learn, and continue to experience the wonder of life.

On the Golf Course

My son, Chris, loves golf, and so does his dad, Holmes. But this past summer my husband was working longer hours and on Saturdays. He also had an injury, so his golf playing with Chris was temporarily curtailed. I had never had any desire to play the game. In fact, I had never been on a golf course in my life, except for a stroll.

But Chris was fifteen and not interested in riding bikes, going shopping, talking, or engaging in any of the other "feminine pursuits" which I enjoyed.

"Do you want to go and play tennis?" I'd ask.

"Not really," he'd reply.

I wanted to find something we could do and enjoy together, so I invited Chris to the driving range. He taught me how to swing the golf club. The next time out, I drove the cart for him (a real treat in the 95-degree heat, since he usually carried his heavy bag and clubs). On that late June afternoon I discovered that I loved being out there on the public golf course (and I didn't even know how to play yet)! Driving the "golf buggy" was like driving a little go-cart. Chris and I sipped sodas, and I relished in the variety of trees we mingled among as we made our way around the fairways. There was a cool breeze off the water, and the sailboats were bright and colorful. We saw a white-tailed bunny, a Canadian goose, an egret. I felt as if I weren't even in the city.

I loved watching Chris work on his different strokes. I served as "official scorekeeper" and found myself not just enduring golf for his sake, but actually enjoying our shared activity. Chris is normally quiet, but he opened up and chatted as we drove around the course. He told me his favorite kind of golf ball and described the basic shots I would need to learn.

"My putting is good, and my driving is awful," he confided.

"Next time we'll practice at the driving range before you play nine holes," we agreed.

During that afternoon we spent together I learned about some of my son's ideas and experiences I might never

23

have heard about at all had I stayed home or followed my usual routine. I may never be a good golfer, but I was an enthusiastic cart driver! I cherish the memories of the outings Chris and I had together, and I hope to learn to play the game in earnest so that next summer, and in times ahead, we can play together.

Time Together

> "Parents are anchors of security to children. Parents of secure children spend more time with them. There is close daily interaction. Close emotional ties are built daily, in small ways. Then any crisis can be handled. Having faith in their parents, they have faith in themselves and others, and life makes sense to them."
>
> Dr. Yamamoto
> University of Colorado

What you enjoy doing with your child may be perusing art in a museum, going hiking or camping, collecting shells, or playing tennis. It all depends on you and your youngster's individual interests. And it's different at five and fifteen as her needs change.

There are a myriad of things parents can do with toddlers and preschoolers, for the great thing about little ones is that for the most part they enjoy doing anything with one (or both) of their parents — cooking dinner, baking cookies, grocery shopping, folding laundry, walking the dog, going to the park and library. At any age, working together can provide opportunities to talk, listen, and just be together.

Ann Manley, one mother I know, sews with her daughter, Monica. They pick out material together, design or alter a pattern, and talk while they work at the machine. Sometimes they do crafts with each other, like stenciling sweatshirts or making T-shirts. Scott and his son, Guy, jog together and play board games. Penny, another mom I know, and Leslie, her daughter, enjoy bicycling together in their neighborhood.

Time together can be spent in doing simple things like cooking, throwing a baseball in the front yard or flying a kite, or on longer-term projects like making a dollhouse or model rockets. My children and I play Ping-Pong in the garage or take a walk to the park. One dad I know had a standing date with his son every Saturday to go to breakfast together. In that weekly time over pancakes, they shared with each other what was going on in their daily lives.

The important thing is to find something you and your child can both share in and enjoy — fishing, music, woodcarving, polishing rocks, going to plays or ballets. Shared activities, no matter how simple or ordinary, help to *build a bridge between parent and child*. Communication naturally flows out of time spent together in an interesting and enjoyable activity.

It's best to start early in looking for something you and your child can do together, so that she won't shut you out when she reaches the age of fourteen or fifteen. We all have duties and responsibilities, but some of our time needs to be spent *building and cultivating a relationship with our children*.

Are We Tuned In?

A recent PTA survey shows that the average father spends two minutes a week with his infant child in focused

25

attention, and seven minutes a week in focused attention with his teenager. Mothers tend to spend more time with their offspring — eight to fifteen minutes of one-to-one time per week. There are a lot of demands on parents' time, but it makes a tremendous difference for a child to know throughout the day, "Tonight I'm going to have some time with just Mom (or Dad) and me."

Focused attention, says Dr. Ross Campbell, in his book, *How To Really Love Your Teenager,* means full, undivided attention which is concentrated on the child or teenager in such a way that she feels loved, that she knows she is so valuable in her own right that she warrants her parents' "watchfulness, appreciation, and uncompromising regard."[4]

When with a child, eye contact and physical affection also build relationship. It has been found that infants respond to eye contact at six weeks of age, but often the only direct eye contact children get at home is when they are being scolded or criticized. Direct eye contact that communicates acceptance, respect, and loving care can help a child feel safe and secure.

Showing physical affection is also important. Studies show that everyone (especially a child) needs at least four to eight hugs a day for good emotional health (and twelve to be a motivated enthusiastic person!). With her emotional needs fully met at home, a youngster will have the emotional energy she needs to become and remain excited about life and learning.

Dorothy Corkille Briggs asks us as parents: "Do you focus so much on doing things *for* your child that you forget to focus on him as a person? Do you rush so fast to bake the cookies, sew clothes, make money for his education that you overlook *him?*"[5]

Direct involvement communicates positively to a child. "Being there for her," not always preoccupied with adult worries and affairs but really observing and listening to her, tells a child: "I love you. You are important enough to warrant my presence and my full attention. You matter!"

Jump In!

It's easy to sit on the sidelines as an observer-parent, but distant from the action, waiting in the car for the piano or karate lesson to be over. I can remember sitting by the pool, worn out from the morning's work, thinking about the typing or the laundry I had to do when we got home, watching my children happily frolic in the water.

One summer, I recall driving to the beach in Ocean Park, Maine, where I was glad to just be able to stretch out in my red-and-white-striped beach chair and read while my youngsters played and swam.

It takes a conscious effort to dive into those cold Maine ocean waves and stay there long enough to get used to the icy water, just as it takes a conscious effort to get involved with our children in their everyday playtime activities.

That day I decided that it was a golden opportunity for me to do something with my children that they truly enjoyed. I reminded myself that it is in doing things together — whether work, study or play — that we get to know our children better and communicate with them, learning from them their hopes, dreams, and disappointments. I realized that in the countless hours of going our separate ways in job, school, scouts, and sports, this might be the only opportunity I would have all day for closeness and personal involvement in my children's lives.

Seize it! my heart said.

It's too cold! my body answered.

But by taking the plunge (after getting used to the freezing water!), I knew that great memories were being built and preserved — wonderful memories of jumping the waves on that sunny day, memories of the sandy peanut butter and jelly sandwiches we shared, memories of the sand castles we built and the sea shells we collected in a coffee can.

It is in such moments of shared activity that a strong, loving parent-child relationship is built. Along with all the other meals, jobs, and events of everyday family life, a solid foundation for the child's self-esteem and motivation for learning and life is being formed and cemented.

Chapter 3

THE POWER OF POSITIVE ROLE-MODELING

"What does *bilious* mean, Mom?" my daughter Alison asked as she was in the middle of reading *A Wrinkle in Time* by Madeleine L'Engle. Propped up in her bed, she was home sick with bronchitis.

"I don't know off the top of my head, but let me run get the dictionary, and we'll see," I replied, racing down the hall with an armful of laundry. A few minutes later I brought our trusty copy of Webster's dictionary to Alison's bedside, and we looked up the troublesome word — "bilious: a. relating to bile, b. disagreeable, bad tempered."

Then Alison read me the sentence in which *bilious* appeared, and suddenly the light went on! She understood the meaning of the word in the context of the story.

"What about *sinister*?" she asked a few pages later. "I'll look that one up!"

Besides providing an opportunity for vocabulary building, when we parents say, "Let's look it up," we make use of a positive, inexpensive, and instantaneous way of fanning the flame of learning in our offspring. It's a small thing, but it shows that we care enough to investigate, that we too are curious about the meanings of words, that we are also learners. Such role-modeling as an enthusiastic learner is a powerful motivator. It sets a pattern for the child to emulate and influences him to become a lifelong learner himself.

The Power of Example

"Actions speak louder than words," Papa always said, and he was right. Words are important, but what sends a more powerful message, and what our children usually imitate, is not our words as much as it is *our actions.* Like it or not, children play "Follow the Leader," and for many years, we parents are the leaders! Our youngsters mirror our attitudes and habits in many areas.

A *model* is defined as "a person or thing which is regarded as a standard of excellence to be imitated." We may not feel like "a standard of excellence," but as Marti Garlett says, children are silent but very watchful observers of what we do. "In fact," she notes, "observing us is the largest part of what children retain about acceptable attitudes and behaviors. Whatever they see us doing, they assume is all right for them too. What they see us do is what they will assimilate as important values for their own lives."[1]

Studies show that whether it has to do with the use of seat belts, tobacco, alcohol, or drugs, one of the main factors that influence children's behavior is their parents' role-model.

For example, according to a recent survey, mothers have the greatest influence on getting children to wear auto safety belts. More than appeals from sports heroes, movie stars, or police officers in safety campaigns, seeing Mom "buckle up" has a powerful effect on a child's safety habits. Of the children in grades five to seven who were surveyed, seventy-nine percent said they believe that seat belts save lives. But only fifty-eight percent said they actually wear the safety devices. Of that group, fifty-seven percent said their mothers regularly wear seat belts, while only thirty-eight percent said their dads always buckled up. The same principle seems to hold true for smoking, eating, television viewing, drinking, and language habits — children tend to do what we their parents *do*, not what we *say*.

We know that fathers have a tremendous impact upon their children's desire to learn and achieve by their interest and involvement in the children's education, and by their own positive role-model as learners.

"Motivation happens more in the process of living with a parent who is intellectually alive and shows excitement over the world of books, ideas, numbers — it's contagious!" says Dr. Arthur M. Bodin.

A love of learning is caught from parents who like to find out, who enjoy learning for its own sake, who seek to add to their store of knowledge simply because it is fun. Let's look at some of the ways you as a parent can contribute to your child's motivation for learning by acting as a positive role-model for him.

Setting the Example

When you go to the library and use the card catalog to look up books on how to make something (as my friend did when she discovered grapevines growing thickly in the backyard of her new house and decided to learn how to make grapevine wreaths), your child learns a little something about where and how to locate information. Maybe you go to a florist friend who is adept at wreath-making, or perhaps you enroll in a decorative arts workshop at a local community college. Your actions may motivate your child to dig for more useful information on the things which interest him. By imitating his parent, he learns how to do research and where to seek instruction when it is needed.

When you write a letter to a great-aunt, or to the editor of the local newspaper, or to a favorite radio or television personality, or when you compose a thank-you note to a special teacher or friend, your child sees the usefulness of writing. He notes that it has value — outside of those worksheets on grammar sentences which he does at school. As your child watches you write, he sees you cross out a word or a sentence, or start your letter again. He begins to understand that writing is a process. He realizes that even adults make mistakes and have to correct their writing so that it will be clear to the person who reads it.

If your child has this kind of role model, he will approach writing in school with more energy, enthusiasm, and a willingness to work harder. He will be more motivated to enter into the process of finding ideas, composing and clarifying sentences, polishing a draft — despite obstacles and disappointments (such as an essay filled with a teacher's red marks) which could easily discourage him and dampen his desire to learn to write.

And when you write notes or an occasional letter to your child, the importance and pursuit of writing skills is made even more personal. Not that every child will become a Hemingway or a Faulkner. But each child can have the motivation to communicate ideas and information clearly and correctly.

My friend Melanie, whose free-lance writing business is home-based, set up two old manual typewriters in her office for her girls, Heather (six) and Lauren (four). Often when Melanie has a deadline to meet or is working on a story, Heather and Lauren type their "pretend" articles and stories and put them in envelopes to "send to editors." Following their mother's example, they also love to dictate stories, illustrate them, and make their own books.

Just as Heather and Lauren like to work as "writers," all children tend to emulate their parents and value the same things they do. One of the main factors that distinguished the homes of every child studied in Delores Durkin's comprehensive 1966 research on early readers was that *the parents were avid readers and led their children by example*.[2]

As you model reading as recreation by reading aloud to your child, you are acting as a powerful force in motivating him to love to read on his own. If you become excited about a new book, so will he. If you take him along on your regular visits to the library to check out books and magazines, or to look up information, you will be doing a great deal to foster your youngster's reading development.

"Let your child see you totally enthralled in a novel. Let him hear you laugh as you read the Sunday paper or a magazine," says Jennifer Jacobson, educational and child development specialist from Cumberland, Maine. "Nothing is so motivating as watching a parent caught in the act of enjoyment. By the time your child learns the magic, the beauty, the adventure of the printed word, he will already have acquired a love for reading."

Telling a child that reading is important while plopping down in front of the television set for several hours of passive entertainment nightly undercuts the message. "Children's brains are not easily fooled," says Frank Smith. "They learn what we *demonstrate* to them, not what we may hope and think we teach."[3]

You can naturally demonstrate to your child the importance of literacy by talking to him while you are doing something which involves reading or writing. You might say, "I'm writing my grocery list so I won't forget the things we need when we go to the store." And when you are grocery shopping, you can read the labels aloud as you choose the brands to buy. Whether you are writing checks, reading the classified ads, taking phone messages, or leaving notes, an explanation of your activity will help your child to see the purpose of literacy in daily life. "The more involved your child is in these processes, the more eager he will be to solve the mysteries of reading," says Ms. Johnson.

Being a Good Role Model

Our role-modeling and our attitude about math and science also have a great influence on our children. We know that the surest way to create a case of math anxiety is to tell a child that you did poorly in math or hated it, implying that he will do the same!

Use every opportunity to integrate mathematics into your child's life in a natural way by discussing numbers and their meaning in everyday activities — on family outings, while playing board games, during trips to the grocery store (try letting the child help you weigh produce, figure the best price on different brands, or calculate the savings on coupons). You will be providing a positive role model and boosting your child's motivation for and skill in math.*

---

*For many more ideas about how to build foundations for math skills, see Chapter 10 in Cheri Fuller's book, *HOME-LIFE: The Key to Your Child's Success At School*. Also see chapters on developing your child's writing, study and organization skills.

Your own curiosity about nature and how things work, your asking open-ended questions, your observations about the season or the weather, your discussing ordinary kitchen science (such as how liquid changes to a solid, or how oil and water mix) can encourage your child's motivation for learning science.

Even in our mistakes we can be good role models. Our willingness to admit our own errors is important. It is vital to talk about the failure, look at it, and learn from it. This attitude carries over into education and affects children's risk-taking behavior, an important factor in the learning process. Home can be a place where the child is provided the support he needs to try new things and to risk making mistakes in order to grow.

Will our children dare raise their hands in class, ask questions of the teacher, try a different strategy when attempting to solve a math problem if the first approach doesn't work? They will, if they are given the confidence they need. If we allow them the freedom to make mistakes, then they won't be discouraged or devastated by their errors. They will be able to admit their lack of knowledge of a particular subject, yet still be open to learn more about it. We can help kids think of mistake-making as a way of learning to do tasks better, and to look upon errors as a natural part of the learning process.

As a parent, how well do I handle failure? How persevering am I in overcoming obstacles, delays, and disappointments in my everyday life? These are important questions to ask ourselves for they represent a crucial factor in our children's school success. In fact, one vital trait of "giftedness" is perseverance. Studies show that persistent children tend to become successful adults. Although there are many inborn personality traits which can affect our children's growth and development, the daily example we set when faced with difficulties or problems will speak much more clearly to them than any "lectures" we might deliver. The fact is that our children's perseverance will tend to mirror ours.

One day, for example, Brian's father told him to stick with his math problem until he had found the solution. As Brian worked, he could hear his father in the garage trying to fix the car radio. He had been at it for a week, taking the radio apart, reassembling it, going to the shop to get a part, then taking it all apart again. Brian learned from his dad's example and his own lessons. He stuck with his math problem and the other challenges he faced into adulthood.

A parent's role-modeling has an important impact upon his child's attitude toward education and work. If the parent values school and feels that attendance and homework are important (and shows it by seeing that the child gets to school every day prepared and on time), then the youngster will tend to share the parent's interest and commitment. (Many teachers are concerned about parents who consistently arrange appointments or make family plans which allow the student to miss school or neglect homework. The message the child receives is that school isn't so important after all!) Attending school meetings, parent-teacher conferences, your child's school activities and sports events, and volunteering in an area in which you have special skill or talent — all these go a long way toward helping your child become a motivated learner.

Parents are models, but so are grandparents, aunts, uncles, pastors, teachers, community leaders, and adult friends — all can have a positive impact on the lives of children. I'll never forget the motivated fourth grader who told me, "My grandfather told my dad who told me that two important things in life are a good name and a good education, and I'm working for both!" A family that values hard work and education passes on those values to children as Proverbs tells us, "Work hard and become a leader; be lazy and never succeed.[4]

We can look around for good role models for our children to get to know and emulate in our extended families, church, and community. People who have interesting jobs and who are excited about what they do are fascinating to children. Invite such a person to dinner and let your child get to know and talk with him. Perhaps you know someone who is doing heart research, or who writes songs, or who is leaving for the Philippines as a missionary. Our son Chris has been inspired by our friend Dr. Warren Low's description of the new knee joint he has invented, and this has encouraged Chris' desire to pursue the field of medicine. Maybe among your acquaintances there is someone who builds sailboats or creates computer programs. There is nothing better for motivating a child to develop his own personal goals than being around adults who have purpose and direction in their lives and who work in interesting, enjoyable professions.

In articles we read in the newspaper or magazines or in programs we watch on television we can point out stories about people who have overcome obstacles and handicaps. We can share about "unsung heroes" who have shown great courage, given extra effort, or contributed to the needs of others. There are people all around us who model positive character traits like loyalty, devotion to duty, compassion, persistence, determination — which can inspire our children.

We can let our children know what we do at work, perhaps even taking them along for a day to watch us at our daily tasks.

One day last summer Alison asked her dad if she could go to work with him. She had gone when he had his own construction office and had enjoyed playing office and sharing a sack lunch with her father. But temporarily he was working in a retail men's clothing store.

"Could I go to work with you and help?" she asked.

"Sure," Dad said.

So Alison dressed up in her Sunday best and went along. While she was "at work," she addressed envelopes to customers for a special mailing. She wrapped gift packages. She gained skills, confidence, and knowledge about customers and the world of work as she watched the tailoring, sales, and paper work her dad did. She even defined some new goals: "I want to work in a store like this one in high school on Saturdays. In fact, I'd like to wrap packages at Christmastime here!" Most of all, she had a wonderful day and an enjoyable lunch time with Dad. Now she likes to go along with him to the building site of a new house.

If we think of ourselves as models, sharing with our children the excitement of learning, both in books and in the many activities of our vocations and homelife, they will have a good foundation for learning and will be more motivated in their own efforts.

Chapter 4

AVOIDING PRESSURE, STRESS AND BURNOUT[1]

Jason's second-grade teacher handed him his spelling test with the grade D written across the top in red ink.

"Don't you think you can do better than this, Jason?" his teacher asked as she posted the scores on the bulletin board.

Jason slumped down into his chair and lowered his head. The bell rang, and the other children ran out to recess, chattering and pushing. Jason chewed his bottom lip as he crumpled up his test paper and stuck it in his notebook.

When Jason got home that afternoon, his mother met him at the door.

"Hi, Jason! How did you do on your spelling test today?"

"I don't know," answered Jason, his blue eyes avoiding her gaze. He unloaded his books and headed for the refrigerator.

His mother sifted through the papers jammed into his notebook until she came to the spelling test.

"A *D*! Jason, this is terrible. How could you make a D?" she frowned, smoothing the wrinkles out of his paper. " 'School'? You mean you couldn't even spell 'school'?"

"I hate school anyway," Jason mumbled between bites of an apple as he quickly made his way out the patio door. "I'm going to ride bikes with Brian."

"Oh no, you're not. You've got only thirty minutes to do your math homework before I take you to karate. And tonight's the scout banquet, and then Dad's going to help you with your social studies project."

Jason stamped away to his room and slammed the door. Through the coming weeks, his grades continued to drop to Fs, and his reading skills were reported to be below grade level. Being grounded from Nintendo, TV, and his bike didn't help. Recurrent nightmares disturbed his sleep, and he woke up tired every morning. Frustrated with his failure, his parents sought help in teacher conferences and from an outside reading specialist. Gradually they began to unravel his problem.

Jason had begun preschool and kindergarten as a happy, intelligent child. The preschool and kindergarten emphasized formal instruction in reading and arithmetic, and his parents were confident that this early foundation would give Jason a head start on school. Both of them were high-achieving professionals who were anxious to give their son the best possible educational beginning. They were eager for him to succeed in school, piano and karate lessons, soccer, basketball, and Little League baseball.

But at eight years of age, pressured to excel in everything, exhausted from lessons and activities every day after school, Jason was a sad-looking, stressed child who had very little motivation for learning. He had trouble keeping up with his papers and books and was failing in his school work.

Jason was the victim of a competitive, overly academic school system, one which placed too much emphasis on worksheets and tests and not enough on "hands-on" activities and concrete learning. He was pressured at home by conscientious, ambitious parents who wanted him to achieve. He was stressed by a lack of free time to play and explore his own interests and develop friendships. So at the early age of eight, Jason was, in fact, burned out.

Here is some advice his parents followed to relieve his pressure, once his basic problem was discovered and isolated:

- Emphasize what is being learned both in and out of the classroom, rather than test scores and report card grades.

  Jason's parents stopped showing disapproval for a low grade; instead, they asked: "Are you having any problems? How can we help?"

- Provide support and structure by helping the student organize his studies and materials.

  Jason's parents helped him organize his papers into color-coded folders for each subject and to keep a calendar with his homework assignments on prominent display in his room. Following through on these carefully planned but limited activities helped to build in Jason a sense of personal responsibility and organization. Kids who are organized have more energy to put into school work and are more motivated to achieve.

- Foster responsibility by allowing the child to make choices, have input in family decisions, and tackle age-appropriate chores.

His parents decided to give Jason the choice of pursuing one favorite activity (he chose soccer) and to drop the others so he could have some unstructured time to play in the neighborhood, ride his bicycle, or have a friend over after school. His dad set aside time on Saturdays to go with Jason to the park, kick the soccer ball with him, and just talk.

Jason was also given the daily tasks of walking the dog, clearing the table after dinner, and taking out the trash. (A child who learns responsibility at home feels more competent and is more motivated and successful in school.) And a neighbor, a retired teacher, met with Jason weekly to build his basic skills through a variety of interesting and creative activities.

Jason's school work gradually improved, and by Christmas of the following year he was reading on grade level. Now in the fourth grade, and a good B student, Jason shows a higher level of self-esteem. He sleeps better and is happier at school, at home, and with his friends. And he thoroughly enjoys soccer.

As schools respond to criticism because of low test scores on achievement tests and American students' dismal showing in comparison with students of other nations, often the tendency is to stiffen requirements, introduce more standardized tests, assign more worksheets and homework — all at an increasingly earlier age. Parents, consumed by a sincere desire to see their children succeed, unknowingly add to the stress. As school and parents apply more and more pressure, many children like Jason are experiencing stress and burnout.*

Children Under Stress

Dr. Darrel Lang, Director of the Center of Health Promotion and Wellness at Emporia State University reports that a survey which he conducted of four thousand Kansas pupils, from kindergarten through third grade, showed that forty-two percent experienced negative stress behaviors including headaches, stomach aches, quick temper, fingernail biting, inability to sleep, short attention spans, and worrying about doing poorly in school. Another study showed that over two million school-aged children are taking prescribed medication to counteract the negative effects of stress and tension in their lives.[3]

"Kids are more stressed out today because our society is more stressful. The fast pace and competitiveness of our society, divorce, both parents working, parents not having time for children, pushing kids too early and too hard — these and other factors contribute to more stress for kids," said Lang.[4]

What Causes Burnout?

Although burnout can take place at any age, it is occurring more and more often in younger children. One of the major causes of premature burnout is the placing of children into pressured academic situations, often as early

---

*There is a "testing explosion" in America. Last year, public schools alone gave over 100 million standardized tests. There is a need for accountability, but when test scores are over-emphasized, the curriculum begins to be controlled *not* by the needs of the children but by more formal teacher-centered lectures, academic skills, and written work for high performance on tests. This puts pressure on kids of all ages.[2]

as age four through six, with hours devoted to desk time, worksheets, and tests. In his book, *MISEDUCATION: Preschoolers at Risk,*[5] Tufts University psychologist Dr. David Elkind warns against rigid preschool and early elementary programs that emphasize rote learning of the "3 Rs," ignores young children's developmental needs, and puts them at risk due to stress and learning problems.

As we have noted, children come into the world eager to experiment, explore, and discover. If they are not over-pressured in their early years, they will continue to be motivated to learn about the world around them and will gain positive attitudes toward learning and the education process.*

Sometimes parents push their preschoolers into formal academic tasks because they feel the early exposure will give them a "head start" toward success. But for many children, especially those who are not ready to read at age three or four, such premature pressure to excel academically causes them to fail or to be labeled "slow." Dr. Elkind has estimated that one-half of all reading problems are a direct result of starting children on a reading program at too early an age.**

---

*Dr. Raymond Moore, a developmental psychologist and expert on the effectiveness of home care and schooling of young children, suggests that many youngsters would profit from delaying formal academic work or institutional schooling until age eight or nine. (See his books *Better Late Than Early, School Can Wait, Home School Burnout,* and others. Write: The Moore Foundation, Box 1, Camas, WA 98607).

**There is no evidence to affirm the current belief that a child will be a better reader or be assured of more success in her school work or emotional adjustment just because she learns to read early. Whether a child learns to read at age three or at age six may have no bearing at all on how well she will be able to read at eleven or twelve.

"We're expecting way too much of young children. It's not natural for little children in kindergarten and first through third grades to be sitting at their desks for long periods doing worksheets and taking tests," says Dr. Carol Kelly, school psychologist in the Jefferson County Schools in Colorado. "A real danger of expecting children to read and do math earlier than they are ready to is that we're setting them up to feel incompetent. Then they feel like failures when we demand so much. The early grades are critical because that is when children's attitude toward school, toward learning, and [toward]...themselves as competent people, is formed."

If children start to feel inadequate at such an early age, they begin to give up and "turn off" of school. They develop a poor self-image and a negative attitude toward learning which may stay with them throughout their school years.

Avoidance of Burnout

How then can we give children a good start on learning without pressuring them into early burnout?

In the early years, children learn best by active participation: by doing things, handling concrete objects, exploring, becoming physically involved. They should be provided a variety of books (from the library and the home) and toys (both "homemade" and "store bought" — a big refrigerator box, for example, can be turned into a great playhouse; blocks of wood which can be sanded by hand are marvelous resources for the construction of all kinds of buildings and bridges).

Encourage your young child to learn and develop on her own. Allow her to play in her own way, for her own amusement — and not necessarily to achieve any predetermined "educational" goals.

"There's no place like home" applies especially to preschoolers. Be aware of the value of your child's time at home, time spent under the influence of your nurture and guidance, time for her to learn at her own pace and in her own manner.

Consider that you are your child's best teacher and that perhaps the rich, loving, supportive environment of home can be a better educational alternative than a structured preschool.

What is important is knowing your child's individual needs and what would be most beneficial to her at this stage of development.*

The Danger of Over-Programming

A second cause of burnout is over-programming. Many children are involved in some type of planned after-school activity every day of the week. Their schedules are crammed with tennis and dancing lessons, competitive sports, and other responsibilities in addition to homework. Structure, rather than spontaneity, marks the lives of many children today. Some structure is helpful, and the activities

---

*If you do decide to look for a preschool program, choose carefully. (See "Providing Preschool Programs Without Pressure" in a later chapter.) A morning program two or three days a week with afternoons at home is much more appropriate and supportive for young children than an all-day program. Or instead, several mothers can get together once a week for a "play group" time for the children on a rotating basis at each parent's home. In that play group setting, children can learn to share, cooperate with others and develop confidence in a small group setting.

themselves are valuable, especially those that are developing a child's strengths. But over-structuring a child's life to the point that she doesn't have time to relax, do leisure reading, daydream, or play, leads to stress and burnout.

Some children seem to be able to handle a hectic schedule, while others are stressed by it, says Dr. Arthur M. Bodin, senior research fellow at Mental Research Institute in Palo Alto, California. He suggests that parents ask these questions:

- Does the child seem to thrive on structured activities?

- Is she eager for scheduled lessons?

- Can she handle this extra involvement, along with her regular homework and family responsibilities, without feeling pressured?

In evaluating any planned activity, parents need to consider whether it is being chosen for the sake of the child or simply to fulfill their own aspirations for him. If I always wanted to tap dance and play musical instruments, but couldn't, I shouldn't force that dream on my children. It's one thing to introduce them to opportunities to learn, and quite another to make those activities compulsory.

What can we do to avoid the over-scheduling that leads to burnout?

- *Find a balance!*

  We need to give children of all ages opportunities for unstructured play, reflection, and rest. The key is to balance planned after-school activities with unstructured time. Every young person needs at least an hour a day of free time.

What if she gets bored? Boredom isn't terrible, and it may give the child a chance to "let off steam" by climbing or swinging in the back yard, working on a hobby, engaging in creative daydreaming, drawing, or even discovering her own interests!

- *Take time with the child!*

Sometimes there are too many things going on in a child's life.

"If you're burning up energy worrying about what's happening with your parents, about tests, and about what you see on television, you won't have much energy left to do a lot of productive learning," says Dr. Elkind. "Everybody's too busy. We all want kids to be instant adults, and they are not; they are growing beings, and *they need adult guidance, protection and support.*"

It is important for parents and children to spend time together in an unstructured enviroment in which the child feels cared about just for being herself, and not for her performance or achievement. Time spent in talking and listening to a child's ideas and feelings helps to reduce stress and avoid burnout. Often, an openness to share a youngster's concerns is best displayed while walking with her to the park, talking before bedtime, throwing a football, or (for me and my son) playing Ping-Pong at a makeshift table on a backyard deck.

- Be aware of the signs of stress and burnout in the child.

Warning Signs of Academic Burnout

Sudden change in attitude and behavior (a child who has been happy and cooperative suddenly becomes hostile and uncooperative).

Declining grades.

Notes from the teacher because of the child's tardiness, absence, poor grades, or unacceptable behavior.

Difficulty concentrating.

Sleeping problems.

Negative statements by child about school or self.

Physical complaints, such as headaches, stomach aches, excessive fatigue, or loss of appetite, without a medical basis.

Lack of desire to attend school regularly; chronic absenteeism.

Evidence of disinterest in and detachment from school.

Anxiety and depression.

Trouble with homework or failure to do assigned school tasks.

One of these signs might not give cause of alarm, but several of them would suggest that the child may be overly pressured by the demands placed upon her at school and home.

Michael, a first-grader I know, was bright and talented and put lots of pressure on himself to perform at top level.

His parents were both high-achievers. Michael was involved in intensive gymnastics practice three times a week for two and a half hours a day, and most of his Saturdays were spent in five or six hours of competition. He had little free time. His teacher told Michael's parents of her concerns about his classroom behavior. He was always worried about his work. He feared making a mistake. He was fretful that something terrible would happen if an assignment was not done at the exact time required. He dissolved into tears if he didn't get a perfect score on every paper. His parents realized that part of Michael's problem was the constant pressure to perform, the competing against himself and others, and the over-structured life he was leading. The result was stress that spilled over into the classroom.

"It's easy to get caught up in the competition," Michael's mom explained. "You can't sit out a year, or everyone will pass you by. The whole program is oriented to produce superstars and winners."

It was a difficult decision, but Michael's parents decided to take him out of competitive gymnastics at the end of the school year. He still works out for fun at the YMCA, with friends, and takes a summer gymnastics work-shop. He has enjoyed participating in a mime group, which makes use of his body and coordination talents. And he is less worried and stressed about school performance, although he works hard and enjoys his work.

"Performance stress is experienced by children as young as four-year-olds," says Arnold Burron in *Children & Stress*,[6] "and it occurs when children are placed into competition of any sort — artistic, musical, athletic, academic — where the emphasis is placed upon *winning* trophies, prizes, accolades, honors, or other recognition, rather than upon doing one's best with the abilities God has given."

As we choose activities and provide resources which meet our children's needs in their early years, being careful not to push them into rigid programs of our choosing, as we find the balance between structured and unstructured time with opportunities for work, play, talk, fellowship, exploration (and even doing nothing at all!), we help them to avoid the pitfalls of burnout and to stay motivated for the adventures of learning and life.

Since grade pressure and overly high expectation are also a main cause of burnout, we will look at some ways to deal with these in the next chapters.

Chapter 5

THE POWER OF POSITIVE
BUT REALISTIC
EXPECTATIONS

Children need to know that their parents believe in them one hundred percent, that they are behind them to support them, that they expect them to do their best. Kids need many positive experiences, small learning successes as well as large ones, at home and at school. But in dealing with our children, we must be careful to balance our high hopes with down-to-earth realism. We need to learn to properly assess and evaluate our children's abilities, strengths, and weaknesses in comparison with others of their age.

"We're proud of all the effort you've put into science this year; we know you can do this project!"

"I'm surprised you missed ten points on that history test because you usually do so much better; you really have an aptitude for history."

Statements like these show our expectations of our children in regard to their learning and achievement. Properly phrased, such *positive* statements have far more potential than most parents realize. Many times spoken (and even unspoken) expressions of parental support, approval, and expectation can be invisible but powerful influences on a child's motivation for learning.

What Are Your Expectations?

"My goal is for Zack to do better and achieve more than I did," said one father.

"I'd like to see my son improve his handwriting, become a good reader, be happy with his friends and school, and develop more confidence," said another.

"I have the dream that my children are going to be wonderful successes, but I won't do the work for them" stated a mother of five. "It's their job to 'duke it out' day to day, and it's my job to stir up their dreams and to encourage them to accomplish goals."

What are your expectations for your child?

The word *expectation* refers to anticipation, to the act of looking forward to something. Expectation implies a hope or belief about what is going to happen or what someone is going to do in the future. But expectation does more than just anticipate; it has a certain amount of power to predict and produce what is anticipated, especially if that expectation is consistently expressed orally.

The more often my son hears me say that I can count on him to spill his milk at the table, the greater his chances for a spill. This example illustrates the power of negative expectation. The same principle works in the positive.

Expectations are what we count on happening. We know that children are very attuned to the expectations of their parents and teachers, and that they tend to fulfill those expectations in many situations, particularly in regard to academic success.

This principle of positive expectation produces dramatic results when applied in the work place or in school. A new supervisor is given a list of six employees and told that they have been especially productive. After a period of time, these workers turn out to be his "star performers." Actually, the six have been picked at random. They succeed, not because they are inherently superior, but because they are *expected* to succeed, because they are treated like winners — like valuable, productive employees. The supervisor, anticipating fine work, is not disappointed.

The same powerful effect of positive expectation can be seen in the classroom. Researchers have gone into public schools at the beginning of the year and tested the students as to their academic potential, grouping them randomly. Their teachers were told that one of these groups consisted of bright "late bloomers" (actually their test scores were not outstanding) who had academic promise and who would become high achievers.

At the end of the term, all the children were tested again. The ones who had been labeled "promising" showed more significant gains in intelligence and achievement than any other group of students in school. Their teachers had expected them to succeed, which had built their confidence in themselves and their abilities. The results also suggested that the teachers' high expectations for these students translated into more positive feedback, created more challenging activities, and boosted the pupils' level of learning and achievement.

Parental expectations are equally strong influences on children. "We know from numerous studies," says Dr. Carol Kelly, "that children usually remain loyal to parental expectations. If they hear positive expectations — that the child will do well, that he can meet the daily challenges, that he will go on to college — then the child does better in the classroom."

In the Heath Family

Expectations and the desire to please certainly played a part in our family. One way I knew that I could please Papa was to do well in school. Education was important to him, and all of us children knew it. Papa didn't ever pay us in money for getting an A, but I could tell that he was happy with a good report card by the warm glow and happy smile that spread across his face. That was reward enough for me.

As part of a large family with six children, how I wanted to please Papa! Mama was an encourager, happy with most of the daily papers we brought home and always ready to add a sprinkling of advice like, "What about your handwriting on this story — were you in a hurry?"

In his quiet, mostly non-verbal way, Papa let us know that he had high expectations for us in school. Although he died when I was only eleven, the power of his positive expectations lived on. Sixth grade had just started when he passed away, and I knew that never again would he be there to preside over the dinner table, take us to the ice cream store, come to open house at school, or carefully examine our report cards.

Papa was gone, but the foundation he had laid in me for the years I was to face ahead in school and in life had already been set. I went on working hard, aiming to learn the most, and do the best in each of my classes. Consequently, I enjoyed school, liked and appreciated my teachers, and discovered some favorite subjects along the way. I had an "I can do it" attitude about school and work, largely because Papa and Mama believed I could do it. The result of their belief was the development of my confidence in myself and my ability (and the more confidence we have, whether in the classroom or on the job, the better we do).

The question is: how can we establish and maintain high but realistic expectations that motivate our children rather than destroy their in-born desire to learn?

Understand the Child's Capabilities

In order to have reasonable expectations about grades and achievement, it is important to gain an understanding of the child's capabilities. Some children will shine in academic work. Others will work hard and never receive accolades (at least not in school). Some youngsters will never be at the top of their class, but will excel in music, sports, or mechanics. These special interests, skills, and gifts must be taken into consideration in setting expectations.

If we have strong expectations for our son to become a lawyer when he dislikes political science and speech and longs to be an engineer so he can design space shuttles, we can easily set ourselves and him up for frustration and disappointment. The wisdom of Proverbs reminds us to "train up a child in the way he should go" in *his* own bent, rather than imposing our ambitions on him.[1]

Testing and evaluation at school can provide clues as to what to expect that a child may achieve in a certain

57

subject such as math or language, but a test is not a foolproof tool or indicator. It only gives clues, not absolute conclusions. Tests can, in fact, be faulty. They should not be used to produce labels to stick on children. Don't let a test limit your view of your child's potential.

More important than standardized or computer-graded tests are your observations about your child: his interests, abilities, talents, and skills. Each child has special intelligence gifts and individual strengths. He also has positive character qualities, and a unique and personal learning style which needs to be respected in the learning process. (In the chapter on building on your child's strengths, I'll provide lots of information about discovering and understanding your child's learning style and intelligence gifts.)

Recognize the Impact of Suggestion

"Science is just too hard for me! My dad told me it would be. He never did well in it either."

Sometimes we as parents and teachers unknowingly reveal our real expectations by suggestions which derail the engine of motivation before it ever has a chance to get going. Negative suggestions produce negative thinking; then negative behavior trails right along behind. Negative suggestions can also produce a "learned helplessness" in which the child doesn't even try because he's so convinced in advance that he will fail. Such "downers" throw cold water on the little spark of motivation for learning which the child may harbor deep within. The result is that he never develops the momentum he needs to keep trying.

Here are some positive suggestions to combat the effect of the negative ones you may have been making to and about your child:

- You can focus on improvement and avoid making suggestions that emphasize your children's errors. Instead, encourage or applaud them for small successes. Rather than pointing out, "You missed five out of ten of these math problems!" try saying: "You got five of these math problems right. That's two more than yesterday; you're really making progress!" Instead of asking, "Why did you miss those three free throws?" you could say, "You made fourteen points — great game!"

A successful and caring Little League coach once told me, "These kids just beam when I point out a little improvement they have made. I always try to reinforce based on improvement, *not* focus on mistakes. Especially the boys who aren't the strongest players or are struggling to keep up with the others need our encouragement. If a teacher, coach, or parent points out any little improvement, it gives the child the *confidence* he needs to try harder."

Give your child a chance for small successes and accomplishments, and his motivation will be boosted.

- You can avoid suggestions that push the child to work for unattainable, unrealistic objectives. Examples of such counter-productive statements are: "You've just got to make a hundred percent on this spelling test"; "You're capable of doing so much better in math; nothing less than an A+ will do!"

A child who is trying too hard to make a perfect score and avoid all error often develops test anxiety. Tensions increase and extra stress is created, causing more failure.

- You can avoid using negative words when making observations, suggestions, and comments. Most kids are exposed to far too much negativism (especially those who have any kind of learning difficulty or problem in school). One study showed that, by the time he graduates from high school, each child will have heard over fifteen thousand negative words, phrases or expressions such as *no, don't, can't,* and *shut up.*[2]

Children hear what they do wrong much more than what they do right. They need positive feedback to counteract the effect of the negatives and to develop and maintain a healthy view of themselves.

Try replacing negatives like *can't, won't,* and *that's incorrect* with more encouraging expressions such as *you're improving, you can figure it out, let's look at the problem this way, you can do it: I'll help, let me show you how,* and *that's better!*

"Love forgets mistakes; nagging about them parts the best of friends."[3] Encouragement works far better than criticism and negative suggestions. It goes a long way toward motivating children for learning — in school and out.

Balancing Expectations

Sometimes children are limited by their parents' low expectations. "I expected nothing from Heather in math because I barely got through it myself," one woman confided. Actually, this mother later discovered that although her daughter was underachieving in the classroom, she had a wonderful aptitude for math.

Often, because of our own limitations or past school experiences, or because of a faulty assessment by a teacher or test, we underestimate our child's abilities. Low expectations can limit any youngster's progress and destroy his motivation.

Consider what your learning experiences were like, both in and out of the classroom, and how they have colored your expectations of your child and your assessment of his capability and potential. But remember, your child is an individual! Beware of limiting his possibilities by allowing him to be unfairly labelled by you or the school system. Many times parents and teachers don't expect much from a child who has a learning problem of any kind, even though he may actually be otherwise very gifted and his learning differences can be compensated for or overcome.

For example, Jason, the son of our friends Debbie and Mike Leslie, suffered a profound hearing loss at the age of nine months as a result of meningitis. Even with his great physical disability, Jason's parents chose to train him auditorially. It was their hope and intention to do everything in their power to mainstream him into a hearing world and to help him make his life as near normal as possible. They didn't want to limit Jason in any way.

It took tremendous commitment, eight years of speech therapy, and extensive work at home, applying whatever they could glean from attending workshops, reading books, and consulting with professionals.

Because of problems with spoken language, one of the biggest difficulties deaf children encounter is learning to read. The average reading level of a deaf adult in the U.S. is only seventh or eighth grade. But the Leslies didn't want Jason to be limited by reading problems. Frequent trips to the library and lots of reading aloud were foundational during his early years. As soon as he was able, Jason also read aloud to his mom, dad, and little sisters, in addition to doing his assigned school reading. When he was home-schooled for three years, he continued his active love of reading. He would read aloud in the afternoon every day while his mother helped him to correct his articulation and speech patterns.

Now fourteen years old and mainstreamed in a regular junior high school and a special program for the gifted, Jason is a terrific reader. At only thirteen years of age, he tested post-high school level in four subjects. In the sixth grade, he enjoyed reading James Herriot's books so much that he finished them in two weeks. He now reads at an adult comprehension level. This past summer he read thirty Louis L'Amour western sagas. He devoured all of Tom Clancy's novels in one month. He is a good communicator and (with the aid of an amplifier) uses the telephone — a huge breakthrough for a profoundly deaf child.

The key to Jason's success, says a speech pathologist, is his parents' involvement and commitment, their high hopes for him, and their refusal to allow his disability to limit his growth and learning. Added to these factors, their patience with Jason and their perseverance over a period of many difficult years resulted in their son's growing up to become a happy, confident teenager and a very promising student.

The Perils of Overambition

Sometimes parents' expectations are so high, a child feels he can never measure up. Three As and two Bs on the report card is not acceptable; he must bring home all As. A grade of ninety-three on a test is not high enough; he has to make a perfect score. In many cases, the parents' own degree of self-worth is dependent upon what kind of showing their child makes in school and sports activities. When parents continually push their youngster to succeed, it may be their own adult self-image and personal status at stake.

As Dorothy Briggs says: "Remember, overambition comes through to children as *non-acceptance*. Unrealistically high expectations mean strong disappointments. And disappointments slam against self-esteem. They turn off the 'go-power' and then the child doesn't even turn on his engine."[4]

When a child fails to meet his parents' unattainably high expectations, he feels discouragement and pressure. "The more pressure students feel, the harder time they have concentrating, and the more distracted and disorganized they are. They become overwhelmed with all the demands and sometimes quit trying." So says Karen Gale, M.A., a reading specialist in Edmond, Oklahoma.

Here are some points to consider if you have a tendency toward overambition:

- Think about your children and list the expectations you have held for each — in school, sports, behavior, etc. Try to objectively evaluate each one individually. Beside each entry write realistic or unrealistic, too easy or too difficult.

- Talk with your older children about what ambitions they think you have had for them. Ask them how well they think they have fulfilled those expectations, and how they feel about them — and you!

Chapter 6

AVOIDING THE PITFALLS
OF PERFECTION

Many high-ability children (especially those of perfectionist parents) become prisoners of their own expectations. They become excessively driven and, more than anything else, fear making a mistake. In this case, the perfectionist child may end up by putting more pressure on herself than anyone else would ever place on her. As one counselor said, when the drive for excellence and "being the best" turns into a compulsive drive for perfection, trouble follows.

This is particularly true in regard to children and their motivation to learn. Perfectionists can end up avoiding challenge and giving up too easily. They may become defensive about what they don't know. They may develop a tendency to focus on past failures and attribute them to low ability. And very often they become underachievers.[1]

In addition, when such children do achieve, often they don't derive any joy or satisfaction from their success because they are always looking down the road to the next goal or challenge.

The Perfectionist:
When "Being the Best" Becomes a Burden

Even as a small child, Sarah was a perfectionist. If she spilled a little ketchup on her dress, she fell apart. If a friend got something out of order in her room, she became upset. In school, she was hesitant about reading aloud or writing down words, for fear she might make a mistake. In the third grade, receiving an A- on a paper caused her to cry for an hour. She became disturbed if her papers weren't "neat enough."

The key to recognizing whether a child has a problem in this area is to notice if she is consistently worried and anxious about perfection. If, in her estimation, a school paper is either perfect or worthless, if a musical piece must be played exactly correctly or not at all, if she must be the best at whatever she does because she fears that otherwise no one (not even her parents) will like her — then she needs a better perspective. Such a child needs to be given reassurance so that she can gain a more realistic view of herself and others.

Countering the Pitfalls of Perfectionism

Here are some practical suggestions to follow in countering the pitfalls of perfectionism:

- Help your child put success and failure in proper perspective by letting her see and hear you admit your own mistakes without acting as though they were major catastrophes or "the end of the world." You might say, "Oh, I goofed on that project, but that's okay; I think I can figure a different way to make it work." Or you could share a story of the time you made a low grade on a test or failed to make the team. This kind of open dialogue about personal imperfection and failure helps perfectionist children realize and understand that other people, even adults, make mistakes, yet still go on leading happy and productive lives.

- Help your child approach new experiences with an understanding that mistakes are a natural part of the process of learning, life, and growth.

Dr. Steve Gold, an Oklahoma City psychologist who works with many young people, says that perfectionists often avoid new experiences because of a fear of failure. They won't try anything new because they hate making mistakes. He suggests talking about and encouraging the perfectionist child to go into new situations with an attitude of: "I'm learning this. I don't know anything about it yet, and I give myself permission to make mistakes while I'm learning."

You can help your child keep her focus on the *learning* aspect of the new activity or skill development rather than on the *achievement* aspect. "I've stopped striving for perfection in everything and started striving for excellence," said one recovering perfectionist teenager.

- Realize that perfectionism often shows up as *procrastination,* especially in school-aged children. When a child consistently delays starting a project or writing an essay, it may be because she wants to produce the perfect work and feels overwhelmed by the enormity and complexity of the task set before her (therefore she doesn't want to even begin it).

Help her break the assignment or task into smaller manageable steps or "chunks" — such as dividing the term paper into three parts and marking the completion of each step with a "victory celebration." Teach the child to set up a series of short-range deadlines to be met one at a time, so she can avoid the stress and pressure of having to take on the entire project or task at once.

- Avoid offering profuse, overdone praise for everything your child does. While praise is positive and needed by children in recognition of the steps they have completed or the accomplishments toward which they have worked hard, extravagant praise can produce a fear of failure and aggravate perfectionism.

Praise needs to be given not just for what a child *does,* but also for what she *is.* Children need to know that they are loved for who they are, not just for what they accomplish or achieve. Youngsters need to be praised for actions and attitudes that have nothing to do with their ability or talent — such as sharing a toy or prized possession, making a get-well card for a sick friend, displaying compassion for someone less fortunate or less gifted, sweeping an elderly person's porch, caring for the family pet.

Word pictures can help to describe the good qualities which a parent desires to see manifested in his child. For example, my friend Joanna praises her daughter Rachel, five, for tending to her puppy and kitten. "You're just like a mother bird with her baby, Rachel; you take such good care of Hugo and Kitty."

- Be careful not to stir up competition or pit children against one another in the family or in the classroom.

Perfectionists tend to be highly competitive anyway, and comparisons only serve to heighten their natural rivalry.

Negative comparisons of children with siblings or friends lowers their self-esteem and increases their fears about not measuring up to parental expectation. Try to affirm each child's worth without making comparisons between her and others. Instead of saying, "You've got to work harder than your brothers and sisters because you're so much smarter than they are," or, "Why can't you do your homework as quickly as Jared does?" try to encourage the child to do her best for her own enjoyment and in her own time. Strive to help each child build the momentum she needs to tackle other challenges by praising her unique qualities and skills, not by comparing them with those of others in the family or classroom.

- Arrange to have the child engage in some activities outside of school which are relaxing and not tied to competition or winning. Encourage her to pursue her own interests and to develop a creative outlet that is not graded, one that is done just for fun and enjoyment. It could be learning a musical instrument, hiking, knitting, playing golf, jogging, or painting — anything positive that the child enjoys doing.

- Encourage and cultivate a sense of humor — in yourself and in your child. Humor can help overcome perfectionism and relieve stress. It allows us to laugh in a friendly way at our own mistakes and avoid becoming overly serious about every event of life.

- Help your child choose a few areas in which she would like to work toward excellence, rather than trying to be number one in everything she does. Sometimes we expect a bright child to be valedictorian of her class, student council president, the most popular student in school, and the best basketball or softball player on the team. *Relax* your expectations. Encourage your child to try to excel in a few important areas, those that matter most to her or those in which she has the most strength, ability, or interest.

The Value of Encouragement

What do we do when we are disappointed in our child's performance or are trying to motivate her to do better? What we find is that children who are unmotivated usually have parents who use negative techniques to get performance, points out Dr. Carol Kelly, a school psychologist in Jefferson County, Colorado. Such parents make threats like: "You're never going to be successful at the rate you're going." "We're going to have to hold you back if you don't shape up." "You never make the grades your brother does." "You're so undisciplined we're going to have to send you to military school."

They use negative techniques like frowning at the child and expressing displeasure at what she is doing or failing to do. Often they get upset at every mistake the child makes. They criticize, withholding their praise or encouragement until the youngster has made some major accomplishment worthy of recognition and reward.

"As much as we know the negative approach doesn't work," says Dr. Kelly, "it's amazing how often parents resort to it when upset with their children's performance."

In contrast, she says, there are lots of studies which indicate the power of encouragement — studies which prove that children who are motivated, who do well, and who keep trying usually are the offspring of parents who act something like cheerleaders, who have positive expectations but are not demanding. They encourage their children by smiles and applaud their efforts appropriately. If a child is unsuccessful in some undertaking, they don't "make a big deal out of it." The parent and child talk about the failure, and even laugh about it. The child is encouraged to try again. Think of the skater who falls down, and then gets right back up and goes on just as if nothing had happened.

Such encouraging parents share in their child's excitement. They cheer her *efforts* as opposed to her *ability*. They help her break down tasks into small steps. They don't wait until their child has learned to play the piano well enough to appear at Carnegie Hall before they offer praise; instead, they celebrate the steps along the way to eventual success. This kind of step-by-step approach makes things much more "do-able" for the child.

"Children have to learn that success comes from hard work, and that it takes time," says Dr. Kelly. "That is why they need lots of encouragement along the way."

Encouragement Versus Pressure

There is a fine line between encouragement and pressure. When we base our acceptance of our children on their school performance or ability to excel in music, art, or sports, this action leads to pressure. The resulting anxiety can lower motivation and lead to underachievement.

But when we balance our "great expectations" with a realistic view of our children's ages, abilities, limitations and needs, when we accept and unconditionally love them for who they are and not for what they do, then they are much more likely to develop the courage and motivation they need to undertake new tasks in school and to keep on learning in spite of difficulties, setbacks and disappointments.

Chapter 7

MAINTAINING A HEALTHY PERSPECTIVE ON GRADES

In recent surveys, teenagers and parents were asked, "What is your top worry?" Their answers: *grades*. Can you believe it? Not drugs or alcohol, not crime or pollution, not disease or death, war or nuclear disaster — but grades!

In a survey of eight thousand fifth- through ninth-graders, youngsters said that their top worry was grades. Another survey questioned parents about their biggest concern for their teenagers, and again the number one answer was grades.[1]

Schools, in an effort to stiffen requirements and improve the quality of education, often increase competition over students' grades. Parents, with a desire for their children to succeed, can unknowingly add to the stress by developing a high-pressure approach to report cards.

Dr. Arthur Bodin, senior research fellow at Mental Research Institute in Palo Alto, California, has been president of an emergency treatment center that answers the calls of young people in crisis situations in the Los Angeles area. He says: "We see regularly an increase in calls around the first grading period, not when school starts. Parents get upset about report cards, tempers flare; kids get worried." A recent national magazine reported that often parents overreact to low grades. More social workers, police, and teachers are seeing that report card time can even trigger a wave of child abuse.[2]

Another problem that crops up along with grade pressure is cheating. A Group Publishing survey showed that seventy-four percent of American teenagers say they cheat on school exams,[3] largely because of a grades-at-any-cost, A's-at-any-price attitude on the part of students, pressure from teachers, and a powerful system of rewards and punishments on the part of teachers.

A Dallas high school principal said: "Cheating in our high school and many others I'm in touch with is at epidemic proportions. And it's not the C or D students who are cheating. It's the top students who are pressured to stay at the top. To keep in the top quarter of their class in a competitive high school like ours may mean keeping up an average of ninety-six or ninety-seven. We're saying, 'You have to keep your grades up to get into good colleges,' or, 'You don't want your class rank to fall.' There's no room for a low grade or missed assignment in any subject."

One middle school teacher said, "I see children striving for grades because they are paid more for an A than for a B. Sometimes they will bargain with me for a better grade, or cheat. The grade becomes more important than the learning."

Children's View of Grades

Good grades are great, of course, but let's get a perspective on grades and what they really mean. First of all, what do children think about them?

Here's what some pupils of different ages had to say on the subject:

Third-graders:

- "If you don't make A's, you don't get to go to college — that's what my mom said!"

- "I like grades when they're good and I get a raise in my allowance."

- "I like to make good grades, and then my parents take me out to eat at Red Lobster!"

- "When I get low grades, I know I can do better, and then I feel bad."

- "Sometimes I feel like burning my report card before my parents see it. I don't like it when I open my report card and have to worry about taking it home to Mom and Dad."

- "Sometimes I worry, like if I might get a C. My parents would ground me."

- "When I get a good report card, Mom says, 'I love you,' and takes me out to dinner to celebrate."

- "My grandpa gives me a dollar for every A+ I make. That's just an incentive to remind me to do good."

- "I'm sort of afraid that I might make a bad grade because then I couldn't be what I want to be. Because you have to be real smart to be what I want to be — a veterinarian."

- "When I grow up, I want to be in the Air Force, and you have to have good grades, *especially in math*, and an A+ in computer to get to go."

Sixth-graders:

- "I get excited about making the highest grade, because I know I'm going to be pleased with myself, and my parents will be happy."

- "I worry about making passing grades, because if I don't, I'll be held back and then I'll be with younger kids."

- "I'm worried that if I get a bad grade I'll be disappointed in myself; it would be embarrassing and my dad would be mad."

- "I'm afraid I'm not going to get enough study time because I always leave everything till the last minute to do, and I'm afraid I'm not going to get it all done. Then I won't live up to my parents' expectations. When I don't get a high enough grade they get mad, but they tell me I can get better."

- "I don't feel pressured about grades because my mom just says to do the best I can and doesn't say get As. And sometimes she quizzes me and helps me study for a test."

Younger children, however, may not have the faintest notion how any grade is figured out or what it stands for. So when parents jump on a child, berating him for bringing home poor grades, the youngster may wonder if grades are something to be feared like a disease. So we need to know what grades mean to our children. If they are not making good grades, they may take the failure personally (as they do most things) and figure they must be bad people. Or they may take their low marks as a form of punishment. Or they may think that bad grades indicate disapproval or a lack of personal regard — that their teacher has a grudge against them or a dislike for them. They may feel ashamed or stupid. Their sense of self-esteem may be threatened when they see that they received lower grades than their peers.

The Nature and Function of Grades

Although report cards seem to exert a big influence on both parents and children, they are actually nothing more than a way to keep records. As Kevin, one of my third-graders said, "Grades are a symbol of how you're doing. If you miss turning in papers, that lowers your grade."

But grades don't tell the whole story. Unfortunately, sometimes we act as if they do! Whether the grade is an A, a B, or an F, it is usually a mixture of the results of test scores, homework assignments, and projects, and reports, along with the teacher's subjective reactions.

Grades can be significant indicators of what part of the material presented in school the child is understanding and remembering. They can also point out a learning gap that needs to be filled. For example, if a child earns a low grade in seventh-grade math, the problem may be that he never really mastered his multiplication tables back in the third and fourth grades and needs help in strengthening some basic math skills. A low grade in English can be partially the result of poor reading skills or a comprehension problem which needs immediate attention. Some low marks are the result of disorganization or difficulty in following directions. Sudden falling grades in the case of a child who has been doing well may indicate burnout, emotional stress in school or at home, or physical problems. So we need to look at what is *behind* poor grades and what difficulties the child may be having.

Grades are important factors for acceptance into honor societies, for receiving an academic award in secondary school, for assuring entrance into certain limited-admission colleges and universities, or for obtaining scholarship funds. It is also true that grades are reviewed along with the application for that first job. But, for all of their beneficial qualities, the plain truth is that good grades do not guarantee success in life.

Good grades are great, but there is only a small amount of direct correlation between academic achievement and success in the real world. There are many people who received low marks in school or college and yet went on to be wonderfully successful in their careers and personal lives. There are some students who worked hard and never excelled scholastically, but who, because of their struggles and hardships, developed the persistence and character necessary for survival and success in daily life. Some of these were people who had behavior problems or reading problems or adjustment problems in school, and later turned around. Some were people who found the rigidity and "cookie-cutter approach" of school a hindrance to their inventive minds or creative bents. Some were "late bloomers."

Recognizing that academic achievement is not all there is to life helps us to keep grades in proper perspective. (If your child has had problems in school or has just muddled along, never winning the "Student of the Month" award, take heart as you read the hall of fame that follows.)

Famous "low-achievers" include Thomas Edison, who was kicked out of school because he was considered ineducable, and Louis Pasteur, who failed the entrance exams to medical school on his first attempt and was labeled a "plodder." Albert Einstein failed several math courses in his academic career. His teachers said he was lazy, mentally slow, and a daydreamer.

Winston Churchill was an embarrassment to his family because he was considered stupid; he occupied the lowest rank in the British school he attended and always had to be the last student to file in at the end-of-the-year services. Authors William Saroyan, Stephen Crane and Pearl Buck were school problems. Another poor student who grew up to be a distinguished adult is inventor Henry Ford. Ray Kroc, founder and builder of the phenomenally successful McDonald's fast-food chain, was a school drop-out, as were the Wright Brothers and Samuel Langhorne Clemens (later known around the world as Mark Twain).

Creativity, willingness to take risks, task-commitment, perseverance, initiative, a burning desire, a consuming interest or an overwhelming passion — many of these factors have a bigger stake in determining a person's success than certain letter grades on a report card.

Don't look upon grades as the primary indicator of your child's potential. What really matters is — what is he learning? Is he being challenged? Is he making enough progress to do the reading, work the mathematical problems, and handle the course material? Is he excited about and interested in any particular subject or hobby? Is there something he wants to know more about? Are his individual gifts and talents being discovered and developed? Is he *learning how to learn?*

Learning effective study strategies is more valuable than just swallowing and regurgitating facts in order to get a good score on a test. For parents, understanding how their children take in, process and apply information — and how to motivate them toward learning so that "the light bulb goes on" ("Oh, I get it!") — is much more important and useful than any accumulation of perfect grades on a pile of report cards.*

---

*Learning style strategies are discussed in Chapter 9.

The Ownership Issue

Another important issue to consider is *whose grades are they?* Often our feelings about grades reflect, as we discussed earlier, more of our own adult aspirations and personal goals than they do our children's. Sometimes parents get so wrapped up in wanting their child to receive high marks that they take over responsibility for the grades (for example, if I stay up half the night doing my son's science project or rewriting Alison's essay). In that case, the parent, rather than the child, begins to "own" the grades. This situation inevitably leads to lowered motivation on the part of the child, because if the parent assumes responsibility for his performance, the youngster has less reason to try: Why care? Why put out so much effort? Mom and Dad will take care of it.

As parents, we need to let our children "own" their own grades and report cards.

We want to be supportive, encouraging, and genuinely interested when our child brings home his grades. Ignoring a youngster's report card or papers shows that we don't care. We need to take an individual approach to reviewing our child's progress (not getting the siblings together to compare results, but sitting down and showing real parental care and concern). We can ask our child:

- "How do you feel about the grade (or grades) you received?"
- "What does this report mean to you?"
- "Do you want to make any changes in how you are studying or organizing the material during the next term?" (Have the child jot down the subject and a step to take or a change to make for the term ahead.)
- "Is there any way your teacher or I can help you meet your study goals?"

If the child has received a lower grade than he is capable of earning, it is time to have a conference with his teacher or to consider the cause of his problem: Is the home supportive of learning? Is learning valued? Are reading and conversation encouraged more than television viewing? Does the child have a specific time and place, and proper materials to study? Is he encouraged to learn and praised for his school work?

Also consider the school environment, including the teaching methods used. (To properly evaluate these factors, it may be necessary to observe the classroom setting while learning is in progress.)

The difficulty may be something as simple as the fact that at school the child sits next to a misbehaving student who is constantly harassing and disturbing him. In some instances the youngster may not be able to see the chalkboard or hear the teacher. All these things affect a child's performance.

Motivating Without Pressure

Here are some tips on how to respond to grades without exerting undue pressure:

- Avoid punishment. Overreacting and applying punitive measures like "docking" an allowance, grounding, and taking away favorite activities (such as sports, television, time with friends), often sets up a power struggle without producing any improvement in performance, says Dr. Arthur Bodin. The child becomes determined to win the power struggle, which can drive him further away from his parents and squelch any desire he may have to improve his grades or performance. Hasty and unwise punishment often causes a child to begin to

81

hate school and the learning process and to develop resentment toward his parents, both of which lower his motivation even more. Children also get caught up in anxiety about the punishment, rather than focusing on their studies and what they need to be learning.

- Avoid criticism. Never make negative remarks such as, "I knew you'd mess up," or, "In our family a D is the same thing as an F."

  These statements only serve to batter the child's self-esteem and throw cold water on the flickering spark of motivation.

- Consider scheduling a parent-teacher conference to look for solutions, especially if there seems to be a problem or if you are puzzled about the cause of the child's poor showing and what to do about it.

- Avoid paying for grades or offering bribes. Some parents offer cars, clothes, vacation trips, and money for a certain grade-point average. But these material rewards tend to work against a child's success and diminish his chances of developing any real motivation for learning.

  "We find the best students are not paid for grades," says Dr. Bodin. "Paying for grades makes the doing of it get interpreted by the child as something he did *for the money* rather than something he did because he loves knowledge, because learning is useful, or because he enjoys the activity. The more he is paid, the harder it is for the child to internalize the value of learning for its own sake."*

And when one sibling is paid for grades and another is not, rivalry and discord are increased in the family.

A child's good report card, achievement, or progress can be celebrated with praise, a surprise pizza, or an outing with someone he enjoys (but make sure that the youngster receives praise and affirmation at times other than just report card week).

Focus on Learning, Not Grades

Instead of focusing on grades, we need to communicate to our children that learning itself is important, that learning itself is valuable. "Too often parents get extremely caught up in the *grades,* and then they say to their child, 'Why doesn't this motivate you?' " says Dr. David Elkind, Tufts University psychologist. "Well, grades are not motivating really, but what is motivating is the whole process of learning and the excitement and challenge of that."

"Grades are kind of dull things to get excited about," he continues. "By emphasizing grades, we may kill children's motivation. So what we should do is to talk with our children about what they are interested in, read to our children, take them to the museum, take nature walks, go to the zoo, see good films. And in our own reading, ask

---

*I realize that many parents do pay for grades, and that this is a controversial issue. Treats, money, etc. can be used on a short-term basis to reward a child. But if we want to help children to develop any *intrinsic* motivation, we need to consider that research has shown that if a child who naturally likes to do something is consistently rewarded or paid for doing it, he begins to work *for* the reward rather than for the enjoyment of the activity itself. This leads to burnout and lowered motivation. There are more rewarding and more effective ways of motivating children's learning, which we will discuss in subsequent chapters.

questions, provide a model of learning and curiosity, and then children can come to that naturally."

So as parents we need to shift our focus to the content of *what is being learned*. That is what the later chapters on boosting motivation for learning history, science, geography and other subjects and for developing literacy skills, are all about. The important thing is not just that the child learns these facts, puts them down on an exam, and gets a mark, for which he receives a stick of candy or a special treat if the grade is high enough!

Edith Schaeffer, author of *What Is a Family?*[24], notes: "What is important is that education is knowledge that *interrelates*. The more you know about history, then the more you understand about when medicine started. What you are learning interweaves with other subjects: art, music, literature. If a parent can supplement and interweave and make more interesting what is going on in the classroom, the child's education is greatly enriched and the child is more motivated."

When we model enthusiasm for learning, share in one another's interests, and encourage our children, whether they are A students or C students, their motivation grows and they have more courage to step out and into new learning situations at school. Most important, whatever their grades, our children need their parents' unconditional love. We need to let our children know that we love and accept them regardless of what grades they make. Our love holds strong and enables them to grow and be motivated for learning.

Chapter 8

THE POWER OF PATIENCE

One of the best ways to balance our high expectations for our children is to show patience — patience in transitions, patience with preschoolers, and patience with late bloomers.

Patience in Transitions

Mrs. Roberts came in with a stack of her sixth-grade daughter's science papers and deposited them on the teacher's desk. "Why is Beth making a B? She's not a B student in science. She made all As in elementary school. Besides, her father is a doctor and was an honor student in science and math."

"Well," began Mrs. Walker, the teacher, "Beth seems to be doing pretty consistent B work in science, with the exception of 2 Cs on daily tests. She's still adjusting to being in middle school and having more responsibilities to keep up with. Her work in math has been average so far. But the area in which Beth really shines and shows great enthusiasm is reading and creative writing!"

Beth's mom couldn't accept the fact that her daughter showed little interest or talent in science but excelled in language arts and writing.

Frequently during the big change from elementary school to middle school or junior high school, children's grades in certain subjects will fall. Their marks in elementary subjects may have been all As because they were based primarily on effort, work habits, neatness, and completed assignments.

In middle school or junior high, however, where courses are departmentalized and where students have several different teachers, children may do very well in one subject and only average in another. It's hard to accept a mark of "Average" or even "Above Average" on a middle school or junior high school report card when your child has made top scores in elementary school.

Teachers in middle school and junior high also focus more on vocabulary learning and skill development in each subject. Reading, memorizing, and digesting of printed material are given new importance, and children's individual abilities and interests begin to be more defined.

The change from middle school to high school also involves a shift in emphasis. In this transition, adolescence is well under way. The middle school environment was more nurturing, with greater explanation and teaching of basic skills. Now more critical thinking is called for. Class time shifts to more lecture presentation and group discussion (so students with strong visual skills who have excelled in the many visually-oriented tasks of early years may experience a drop in grades if they haven't developed good listening, note-taking, and verbal skills necessary for classroom participation). There is less spoon-feeding of facts.

"This is high school now," teachers say. As one freshman student remarked, "In physical science my instructor gave me a sheet with first semester assignments, an outside reading list, and a test schedule. I felt like I was on my own."

If your child has failed to develop any particular study skills along the way, this can be a hard time for her.

How can we as parents help our children with these difficult transitions? We can be calm (which is not always easy!) and *patient* as our children learn the new skills required of them, find their footing, and make the adjustments needed to survive in the new middle school, junior high, or high school environment. (The opposite of calm and patient is "excitable, irritable, hysterical, high-strung, and hot-headed," qualities which will only make the situation worse.) We can be encouraging if the results at the end of the first grading period are not what we or the child had hoped. We can avoid demanding that the child do perfectly in everything, understanding that she may do better in some classes than others. We can provide support by helping her to stay organized and keep in touch with her teachers.

If you find that there is a lot of tension and conflict in your household around report card time because of your unmet expectations for your child, it helps to reassess your child's abilities, recall the transitions she may be going through at the moment, and focus on the learning process and not just on grades.

Patience With Preschoolers

Sometimes as parents we expect far too much emotional and mental maturity of preschoolers and early elementary-age children who are larger physically or have

87

a lot of verbal ability and "sound older" due to watching television and imitating adults or older children. Often we expect the behavior of younger children to match that of their older siblings. But our expectations need to be based on an understanding of our child's level of development. We need to learn to be patient with our younger offspring, seeing them at the age and stage they really are, not "just like big brother," not like little adults. We must avoid hurrying our youngsters to carry more responsibility or produce more achievements than they are able.

Dr. Louise Bates Ames gives us some sound advice on this point: "Respect individuality. Respect immaturity. Respect your child for what he or she is now, as a preschooler. There may never be a happier time."[1]

Being patient does not mean being passive or permissive, says Dr. Ames. As parents, we love, discipline, teach, and correct. But knowing what is and what is not normal and expected behavior in preschoolers and children of different ages helps us *not* to be too hard on ourselves or the child for her displays of childish irresponsibility or immaturity.

"Knowing what is reasonable," adds Dr. Ames, "also means that though your hopes and goals will remain infinitely high, you will, hopefully, be able to wait." And waiting, she says, is a very active thing indeed.

"It often takes a good deal of energy to restrain that impulse to push, shove, suggest, insist, and even punish for poor performance or lack of performance."[2]

Patience: a wonderful gift we give our young children which helps them to be enthusiastic and motivated as they learn and grow, and as we relax and enjoy them right where they are.

Early Childhood Programs That Don't Push

Here are some important factors to consider when looking for suitable preschool, kindergarten, or early elementary schooling for your child:

- Is attention given to children's individual development and learning styles?

- Is the environment warm, loving, and supportive?

- Do teachers seem to understand and enjoy the children?

- Are there opportunities for learning through exploration, experimentation, observation, building, dramatic play, and hands-on activities?

- Are the children free to learn and develop at their own pace — or is there a rigid pre-reading and math program?

- Is the emphasis on learning by doing — or on the completion of worksheets and tests?

- Is there individual freedom of development and expression — or is there a competitive atmosphere with an emphasis on earning grades and getting the "right" answer?

- Are there opportunities for children to be active and to use their large motor skills in the learning process — or are they required to sit in desks and accomplish tasks appropriate for older children (i.e. those demanding lots of close work dependent upon visual and fine motor skills)?

- Is the children's time spent on integrating oral language, writing their own stories (by dictation or invented spelling) and listening to reading for pleasure — or is it devoted entirely to isolated skill development such as penmanship?

Always make sure you visit and observe any school in which you are considering placing your child. Don't base your decision on someone else's experience or your neighbor's opinion as to which program is best suited for your offspring.

My husband and I learned this lesson the hard way. Our oldest son was in a very low-key, two-morning-a-week church preschool in Waco, Texas, which he really seemed to enjoy. When we moved to Tulsa, Oklahoma, we began to ask around for a good preschool. We were told that the best was Betty Davis Preschool (not its real name, of course). Being young and ignorant, we visited with the director of the school who told us how wonderful her program was and briefly showed us around the building and grounds. We enrolled Justin and I dutifully took him twice a week, thinking that it might help him form some friendships in our new community.

It was not until the last week of the term, when parents were invited to come and observe, that we realized our mistake. The children were aggressive; none of them shared anything or played with our son. The teachers ignored him, instead of helping him become part of the group. The atmosphere was competitive — so much so that my husband and I both got a little sick just watching what was going on.

"No wonder Justin didn't seem excited about coming each week," we exclaimed almost in unison.

The moral is: take time to go and investigate the school thoroughly. Spend at least one morning in observation. After your child has been enrolled for a few weeks, schedule a follow-up visit. See how well she is enjoying the program, progressing in her learning and development, and interacting with both teacher and classmates.

The Value of Play

One mother I know, who has four children, told me how much it irritated her when her children spent time playing. She was bothered by the mess that always seems to accompany making a tent out of a sheet or playing house with Mom's kitchen utensils. She was also upset because when her children were playing, they didn't seem to be involved in *constructive learning*.

But children need early years of play. In fact, *for young children, play is learning.* Dr. Ames says playtime aids a child's growth. It embodies a high degree of motivation and achievement. It offers opportunities for the child to make decisions and solve problems. It offers freedom of action and contains elements of adventure. It establishes a strong base for language building, because vocabulary grows as the child engages in play. Play also provides opportunities for the child to learn to relate to other people.

Unfortunately, we see more and more competitive team sports at younger ages. But "play *is* the young child's world of sports," says Dr. Ames.[3] Children climb, run, push, pull, build, and exercise their large muscles. They use their minds and stretch their imaginations by making up their own games. By manipulating small objects, like toy cars and puzzle pieces, they develop and improve their fine motor skills.[4]

Young children learn by seeing, touching, and engaging their senses. They learn more about math by counting concrete objects like beans or bears than by struggling with abstract symbols on paper. They develop conversational skills and enlarge their creative imaginations by engaging in spontaneous "let's pretend" games (ones which are their own idea rather than a parent- or teacher-directed activity). They learn to reason, solve problems and cooperate with others by building a backyard fort. They learn about the reading-writing connection by dictating a story to be recorded on paper by parents or teacher. They become motivated to read by hearing interesting stories read to them or told aloud at home and at school. Given the materials and time, children follow their natural curiosity and investigate causes and effects.

Crayons and paper, blocks, paints, sand, plants, dolls, cars and trucks, modeling clay — these are the stuff of a young child's world of play and learning.

But we can encourage the precocious child who shows an early interest in reading, writing, and numbers (as long as we are careful not to push reading too early just because the curriculum demands it). If, while she is in a playful, curious spirit, a child should happen to learn to read, that's great, said one educator. I agree! How exciting to decode for herself the meaning of the mysterious symbols on the printed page! I remember the fun I had as a child deciphering the messages on the streets and highways of Dallas, Texas. I would play school at home, practicing the letters I had seen and drawing pictures on the blackboard. It didn't matter much then that I sounded out "salon" as "saloon." Then I moved on to sounding out words I discovered in the books my sisters left lying around the house. In this way, the wonderful and exciting world of words opened up to me in a beautiful and natural way.

As caring parents and teachers, with a little planning and effort, we can provide numerous opportunities and resources for the early reader to continue to grow in reading skill.

Patience With Late Bloomers

> "Patience is the art of hoping."
> Vauvenargues[5]

One of my favorite children's books is *Leo the Late Bloomer* by Robert Kraus.[6] The main character, Leo the little lion, can't do anything right. He can't read (the wonderful illustration shows how sad Leo is about this situation as he sits in the tree bewildered by the written page before him while all the other animals are happily reading). He can't write (only scribble). He can't draw (like the rest of the creatures of the forest). And he eats sloppily (while all of his friends eat neatly, of course).

"What's the matter with Leo?" asks his father.

"Nothing," replies his mother. "Leo's just a late bloomer."

"Better late than never," thinks Leo's father.

The rest of the story goes on to describe how every day and every night Leo's father watches him for signs of blooming. He watches and watches, and still Leo doesn't bloom.

Somewhat discouraged, Leo's father asks, "Are you sure Leo's a bloomer?"

"Patience," answers Leo's mother. "A watched bloomer doesn't bloom."

So the snow comes, and then spring, and Leo's father is no longer watching. But Leo is having a fine time playing and exploring and growing!

"Then one day, in his own time," the author tells us, "Leo bloomed!"[7]

And we celebrate with Leo as he now can read, write, and draw with a flourish. He even eats neatly. And when Leo speaks, it isn't just a word; it's a whole sentence. And the sentence is, "I made it!" as on the last page we see Leo, his dad, and mom hug one another. And we want to hug them too!

The message of this marvelous book is for each of us as parents — to have patience with late bloomers, to believe in them, and to know that, like Leo, in their own time, *they will bloom*. They will learn, they will develop, they will become all that they can be.

We can have faith in our late-blooming children, in their gifts and abilities and individuality. And we can make sure that they have the support, nurture, and encouragement they need both at home and at school while they are growing — *before* they start blooming. We wouldn't impatiently stamp our feet, insisting that our prize petunia plant bloom before it is ready. And neither must we demand that our children bloom prematurely.

Dr. Thomas Armstrong advises that we think of late blooming in broader terms than just reading, writing, and arithmetic. "Some parents may need to stop equating blooming with success in the three Rs. For a few children, especially bodily-kinesthetic or spatial learners, blooming in life may have more to do with achieving success in artistic, mechanical, or athletic areas."[8] One child may bloom as an actor or a dancer; another may bloom as a landscape designer or musician.

Tim had a natural ability to figure things out. Although his degree of academic achievement was not like that of his sisters, his parents didn't "put him down." They didn't compare or limit him because he didn't become an accountant like his dad or his big sister. Shortly after high school, Tom landed a job as an electrician and went on to earn his apprentice and journeyman's license. He gained a lot of confidence and skill as he continued to develop his natural mechanical abilities. Now he has an excellent job as an engineer.

Randy was one of six children, and suffered from a speech impediment from birth until five years of age. He had problems in school and was not good in math, science, or English. But he started whittling at age four. Although he experienced frustration and rejection at school, some kindly next-door neighbors, an elderly couple, accepted him, spent time with him, and praised him for his unique woodcarving ability. Today Randy is a prominent Southwestern sculptor.

Broadening our definition of "blooming" paves the way for our children to develop in the pathways of their own talents and according to their own timetable.

When Justin was in his early school years, he lacked some maturity for school learning. His auditory memory age and reading comprehension age were behind his chronological age. He had also missed a lot of school due to illness. An extra year in first grade helped him gain more solid reading skills and he made tremendous progress. In his elementary years, he didn't garnish any academic awards. Throughout junior high and early high school, he worked hard, developed valuable study skills, and learned to be organized with his assignments and chores. He struggled in some courses, and always had to put out extra effort to succeed.

But in the tenth and eleventh grades in high school he became extremely motivated. He made a 3.5 grade-point average one semester and enrolled in several honors courses in his senior year. He was fascinated by his high school college-level course in business management. He was sparked by ideas and philosophy, discussion and debate. He has strong interpersonal skills and writing ability. Now he looks forward to college and hopes to go on to law school. His grades are the highest they have ever been. After years of encouraging children through the hard times, what a joy it is to watch them "bloom."

The old saying may be true that the early bird gets the worm, but late bloomers can have great futures too. Gary Decker is a good example.

Gary began his education early, at five years of age, in a small school in Kansas. His older sister, at the top of her class, gregarious and popular, was "a hard act to follow." Gary did average work in elementary school, and made Cs and occasionally Ds in high school. He was small for his age (only five-three when he was a senior), so he had few opportunities to participate in sports. His high school band teacher took an interest in him, and after music lessons at the leader's home, he and Gary would sit in front of the fireplace, eating peppermint ice cream, and listening to classical music.

During Gary's last year of secondary school, the school counselor said that she and the staff didn't feel that he was "college material," but his parents sent him to summer school after graduation. Since he did passable work there, they sent him on to Wichita State University, where he played in the marching band and majored in music. By now he was six feet tall.

Gary made average grades in college and received a degree in music education. But after completing his college studies, Gary decided he didn't want to make a career in music, although he still had no clear direction for his life's work. For a time he served on a campus ministry. Later he got married and began working as an orderly in a hospital. There the chief general surgeon became his best friend and mentor. After training as an operating room technician in another state for two years, Gary decided he wanted to be a doctor.

It took two more years of college to get all the science courses he needed to apply to medical school. During those two years of study, Gary made a perfect 4.0 grade-point average, pulling up his overall average considerably. He was almost twenty-nine years old when he began his medical studies, which lasted four years. Then came five years of residency. At the time of this writing, Gary is a licensed physician in his third year of practicing surgery.

Gary, a classic late bloomer, didn't shine in elementary school, junior high school, high school, or college, but later he became an excellent surgeon. Why was he able to go so far? Because it had been instilled in him that hard work, perseverance, and a willingness to delay gratification were essential ingredients for making something of himself. And his parents and his wife continued to believe in him and to patiently and lovingly support him in his efforts.

As parents, should we do any less for our children?

Chapter 9

MOTIVATION BOOSTER #1: BUILDING ON STRENGTHS AND INTERESTS

Finding and building on individual strengths and interests is a great way to boost motivation for any child, but especially for the student who is experiencing problems with school work. These strengths and interests can be discovered and built upon by recognizing the child's innate intelligence gifts and by understanding and capitalizing upon his individual learning style.

When we highlight the positives (what the child can do well, what he's good at and interested in) rather than the negatives (his slowness in math or reading, or his weak auditory memory), we help the child to compensate for his weaknesses and develop confidence in his strengths. As those strengths are recognized and reinforced, the child gains momentum. He becomes more motivated to tackle challenging tasks at school and to keep on trying in spite of difficult problems or discouraging obstacles.

In regard to your own child, think about these questions:

1. What are his interests? Often these are the key to success in school and in life.
2. What is he skilled in or talented at?
3. What are his strong character traits?
4. What are his learning strengths?

Dr. James Dobson says that one of the best ways of instilling self-confidence is to teach methods by which children can compensate.[1] This is especially true in learning, in gaining skills for life based on the child's unique personality and individual learning style.

Learning (or cognitive) *style* refers to the primary way in which a person learns. Due to inborn characteristics, different people depend upon different channels to take in and process information.

Learning Differences

Some people have a natural talent for visual learning (learning through seeing, reading, deciphering diagrams and studying charts) which helps them excel in areas like spelling, puzzle-working, and geometry. A person with visual strengths has a sharp memory for things he sees, almost like a photocopy machine in his brain. Thus, he memorizes easily what he reads, has a good sense of direction and orientation and is often able to navigate well on the highway or in city traffic, especially after studying a map of the area or city.

Other people learn better auditorially (through listening and verbalizing). Their gift causes them to do well in areas like following oral instructions, participating in group discussions, and learning to read phonetically. It is as though the auditory learner has a tape recorder in his head taking in and storing up bits of important information.

Still others have a talent for learning kinesthetically and tactilely (through touch and movement). They seem to have a special control tower or computer which regulates and times their movements into a special rhythm or coordinated pattern. They learn best by doing. They excel in athletics, mechanics, dentistry and engineering. *Some children are a blend of styles, a combination of visual, auditory and/or kinesthetic and have strengths in more than one modality.*

In any school situation there are lots of learning differences (a much better term than the word *disabilities*): the imaginative student who has trouble following oral instructions, the talented athlete who may have great difficulty with reading, the child who is skillful in visual arts but who has a hard time handling symbols (such as those used in chemical formulas and algebraic equations).

What Kind of Learner Are You?

It helps when parents are aware of their own personal learning style. If you don't know what kind of learner you are, all you have to do is picture yourself in a pressure situation and notice how you react.

Imagine, for example, that your employer comes in unexpectedly and says to you, "Here is a new piece of equipment we will all be using in the office from now on. Take the rest of the day and get acquainted with it because tomorrow you will be tested to see if you have learned how to operate it correctly. This is a part of your employee evaluation."

How would you approach this challenge?

Would you sit down and carefully read the operator's manual and study the enclosed charts and diagrams?

Would you look for someone to explain the operation of the machine to you orally, watching as your instructor describes each piece and demonstrates its function?

Would you start right in working with the machine on your own, figuring out how it is constructed and learning to operate it for yourself through personal experience?

Or would you prefer to combine two of the above approaches? If so, which ones?*

The way you would prefer to go about learning a new subject or technique in such a pressure situation is a good indication of how you learn best. If you would prefer to learn by reading an operator's manual, you are primarily a visual learner; if you would prefer to have someone explain the operation of the machine to you, then you are an auditory learner; or, if you would prefer to learn by operating the machine yourself, then you are a kinesthetic learner or you may be a blend of visual/kinesthetic or other combination.

In this situation, I would want (and need) someone to explain the machine to me (to be patient enough to show me how it works, answer my many questions, and re-explain the whole operation several times). This reveals my auditory tendency and strengths. If I had to depend upon written instructions, I would want to read them aloud in order to understand them. Abstract diagrams don't help me very much; what helps me most is a good instructor.

How a person learns also depends a great deal upon the nature of the material or task. If the skills and information to be learned are very abstract, outside of what

---

*This method of learning style determination was suggested by Dr. Phyllis Agnes, a learning specialist and consultant in Fort Wayne, Indiana.

I can easily relate to in my everyday world, then I will need a clear explanation, someone to walk me through the process, and utilization of all the learning channels available to me (seeing, hearing, and doing).

Just as you and I have different strengths and weaknesses in regard to the way we gather information and develop skills, so do our children. A great way we can help to boost their motivation to learn is to recognize, understand, and build upon their individual style of learning.

When parents understand their children's different learning styles, they can eliminate some of the homework conflicts which arise so often, especially when the learning style of parent and child differ: "I've told you a dozen times how to solve that problem; why can't you get it?" "Look, the book explains that passage; read it for yourself." "See how easy it is to operate this thing; you're just not trying to learn."

As one mother said, "My son and I see things differently. When he got stuck with math problems, I would re-explain them, but it didn't help. Math was still Greek to him. We both ended up frustrated. So now he avoids asking me for help."

If we are aware of learning differences, we can help our children develop effective study strategies that *work for them* and which they can use when they encounter a learning difficulty, especially in a pressure situation such as an upcoming test or deadline. Knowledge of a child's particular learning style, and his unique strengths and weaknesses, can give us the tools we need to help him become an active learner instead of a passive one.

Note that in the examples that follow, it helps to introduce information through their strongest modality (visual, for example) and reinforce with auditory and kinesthetic activities. If your child is a blend, combine learning strategies. Kids need opportunities to see, hear and do in the learning process!

Children With Kinesthetic Strengths

Karen

"The principle that helped us the most as we have parented Karen (who has a strong kinesthetic bent) is, instead of going with our first reaction when she doesn't seem to understand or doesn't have a clue about what's going on, and saying, 'Why aren't you paying attention; how could you be so stupid?' " said Gretchen Passatino from Costa Mesa, California, "instead is to think, 'How are you thinking about this?'

"We've done two things since Karen, now nine years old, was little. One is to understand how she learns, and the other is to teach her in those ways.

"Karen now learns physically and tactilely better than any other way. When she was four years old, she was having trouble distinguishing between the letters of the alphabet. She had wooden letters and she liked them, but to her there was no significant difference between P and D, W and M, etc. So I took inexpensive fabric remnants of different materials and made two-and-a-half-foot tall shapes of all the alphabet letters. Karen played with the soft, stuffed, brightly colored letters. She could manipulate them with her own hands to see how if you turn the letter upside down and backwards, it's a lower-case B, and if you turn it the other way, you can feel it's a P. Playing with these letters, she learned the alphabet and began putting letters together to make simple words."

Karen attended a parent-participation preschool in which there was one parent or teacher to every four children. There were also lots of "hands-on" activities — working with clay, finger-painting, playing with a sandpan, using manipulatives. Karen's teacher said of her, "She will always excel in what she does with her hands." She was right. Karen could make a perfectly formed cow out of clay while the other children made shapeless lumps. But when she was asked to draw a circle, Karen's line would wander of the page. Yet she could take a piece of clay and roll it into a rope, then connect the rope and tell everyone it was a circle.

Her parents read a lot to Karen at home. Today she is a really active, energetic child. By doing things with her in their everyday life, her parents seemed to help her learn best. For example, while driving, they would say to her, "Karen, watch for the Fair Drive sign and tell me when you see it so I can turn there." She learned math best by handling concrete objects around the house. When Gretchen was baking, she would say, "Karen, let's make some cookies; show me three and a half cup measures of flour." She would have Karen show her the number three on her fingers, and then ask her to measure out three cups of flour.

Karen counted rocks and little blocks; it seemed that the rougher the texture of an object, the more it held her attention. Later, in the third grade, she couldn't master her multiplication tables by sitting down, repeating them to herself, or reading them silently. She learned them better while walking around the house or when quizzed by use of flash cards while riding in the car.

Her parents have tried to be aware of her talents, and to give her outlets, like gymnastics practice, for her boundless energy. She is also a great help with her younger brother. She taught him to tie his shoes, and to ride his bike without training wheels at age three. She has a great command of her physical body and natural ways of patterning others to help them learn skills.

"Parenting a kinesthetic child is really hard work, though very rewarding," says Karen's mom. "Karen is a straight A student, and very cooperative and happy. It takes a lot of time to be more involved with her instead of saying, 'Just learn your multiplication tables yourself.' She has a marvelous attention span for things she can be actively involved with. It takes paying attention to the child and a big investment of time, but it's fantastic."

Jamie

Jamie had trouble studying for his fourth-grade spelling tests. The day before each quiz, his parents would dictate the spelling words orally and he was supposed to spell them aloud. He would always seem to know them, but on the test the following day he would misspell five to seven words out of thirty. Jamie's dad knew his son was bright and became upset because the youngster wasn't making higher grades. So he insisted that Jamie write each word five times on narrow-ruled paper. Jamie hated it. By the third or fourth time, the words were coming out wrong, and he was frustrated with having to stay within the small lines.

After Jamie's mom and I talked about his learning strengths, she made some changes. She got a big blackboard which they mounted on the wall in the playroom. In the kitchen she put up a white chalkless board with bright felt-tip markers.

To study his spelling words, Jamie first practiced writing them by syllables in large letters on the big blackboard. Then when he was ready, his mother dictated the words to him in the kitchen as he took a practice test using the felt-tip markers to write his answers on the white board. By following this routine, Jamie usually got a hundred percent on his spelling quizzes.

"He's so much more motivated now when he comes in to start on Monday afternoon," his mom says. "He used to begin the night before and dreaded spelling tests. He decided to do the first ten words on Monday, the next ten on Tuesday, the last ten on Wednesday, and to review them all on Thursday and take a practice test. On his own he starts his study process early instead of saving it until the last minute."

Breaking his study into small, manageable "bites" of learning, Jamie has retained much more and has enjoyed a boost to his self-esteem. He also has a much more positive attitude toward his homework. Most of all, he has learned more about himself, and has discovered, "It's okay to be active when I learn; I don't have to do it like Christie does who silently studies the spelling list and gets an A."

As practice in preparation for the Geography Bowl, Jamie's mom fired off questions from the couch, while Jamie bounced the Nerf basketball and shot a basket with each answer.

Strategies for Promoting Kinesthetic Learning

- Buy a big chalkboard or a large white chalkless board with markers for the child to use to practice spelling words, math, etc.

- Encourage lots of drawing in preschool years; let the child dictate stories and make them into books.

- Make use of multisensory reading and writing materials (like sand on a cookie sheet to trace letters). When introducing a new word, show it with an illustration, then have the child draw the word in shaving cream, colored salt, chocolate pudding or dry Jello mix (in the latter two instances, he may lick up the word once he has recognized it). Then he can write the new words on the big chalkboard or with finger paint. Help him to sound them out as he writes.

- Utilize alphabet letters, like those Karen's mom made for her.

- Use concrete materials found around the house (like Cuisenaire rods, beans, muffin cups) for the child to count, add, subtract, and multiply in order to learn and practice his arithmetic.

- Allow the child to bounce a basketball, clap his hands, or march around the room while practicing rote material such as math facts or multiplication tables.

- Make up a cheer for spelling words; pantomime vocabulary words and then let the child guess the correct answer.

- Remember that it helps the kinesthetic child to retain information better if it is set to song and movement.

- Provide a puzzle map for the child to take apart and reassemble to learn geography facts (like the states of the union or the nations of Europe).

- Allow the child to "play teacher" (i.e. stand in front of a chalkboard and teach the material to *you* or a sibling just before the test).

- Provide the older child a typewriter or word processor to use in writing stories and doing school assignments.

- Make sure your kinesthetic student learns to take good notes by the time he reaches junior high school. He may need help with listening skills with games like "Twenty Questions" (or some of the suggestions in the "Learning to Listen" section of the following chapter). He may also need help with organizing his books, possessions, and assignments (which should be kept on a daily calendar).

Although children with strong kinesthetic skills often have the most problems in school, they can excel and succeed when their parents and teachers perceive and tap into their special learning channel.

Learning Auditorially

Jade

On the fifth-grade level in a home school, Jade was finding the repetitive drill for spelling and math sheer drudgery. After her mom began to understand her daughter's learning style (strong language skills and auditory strengths), she tried a tape recorder with a fill-in-the-blank tape which I had suggested. Jade recorded her metric and measurement assignments and reviewed them nightly by playing the tape over and over until she could repeat the answers perfectly. She also made great progress by putting her history chapter reviews and spelling words on tape and then listening to it and spelling the words out loud.

"Jade has enjoyed schoolwork much more, and has been a lot more of a self-learner, taking initiative for mastering the information she needs to know," says her mother. "It also took away much of the tension between the two of us which had developed from my going over and over the information with her. I still teach and guide her learning process, but the skill drill and studying for tests she does on her own. The tape recorder has just become a part of our natural learning routine, and all my girls enjoy it."

Jade's little sisters also use the recorder for play and learning. They record a story onto tape, each reading a part. They make up stories and record them for each other, and play them back over and over. Jade records stories and books for her sisters to play at nap time.

And, like many auditory learners, Jade loves to write. She has a blank, cloth-covered book in which she writes her own stories.

Justin

As a junior in high school, our oldest son, Justin, had to memorize a long poem, which was made doubly difficult because of its obsolete language. He had three weeks to learn every word of the poem, pass or fail. The first week he read over the piece many times, and when Friday came, he could recite only two of the eight stanzas. The second week was the same; he studied the poem in his book, but had only memorized three stanzas. He had one more try.

Before the third week, Justin recorded the poem on a blank tape and played it on his car stereo while driving back and forth to school, to his job, and to ski team practice, repeating the lines along with the tape. When Friday came, he knew the entire poem word for word.

What was the difference? When Justin used his auditory verbal skills, he learned and retained much more.

Justin also studies best with a study group in several subjects. He and four other boys get together before an exam to discuss possible test questions, list answers, and make up practice quizzes.

In a slump while trying to learn Spanish vocabulary words, Justin put the English words on one side of an index card and the Spanish words on the other side, then recorded both. He practiced with the tape and carried the cards in his pocket to refresh his memory during the day.

Justin's sister, Alison, tapes information and occasionally sets it to music and a beat to help her remember — even geography facts: "Chile on the left, Brazil on the right...." It also helps her to write out study sheets and make study cards.

Strategies for Promoting Auditory Learning

Most students of all ages need strategies to study and learn, to gain confidence, and to compensate for weaknesses.

Auditory learners often have a hard time filtering out sounds. They may be able to focus on their reading or study until the telephone rings or the heater fan comes on, then their concentration is broken. For them a quiet place to study is a necessity.

Some of the best ways to help the auditory learner include the following:

- Talk with the child as much as possible.
- Provide him with lots of opportunities for storytelling and books, records, and tapes of the spoken word and music.
- Create opportunities for writing pen pals, keeping a journal, helping get stories and poems published in children's magazines, and making books.

- Quiz orally on material to be learned or use a fill-in-the-blank tape for review. When Alison used a tape to memorize the main rivers and mountain ranges in all seven of the continents of the world, she brought her grade up from a D to an A. (As a good example of an auditory learner, just reading over the information and looking at maps didn't get the job done for her.)

- Have the child play a card game like "Concentration" in which pairs of vocabulary or study cards are turned face down and then correctly matched as the game progresses. (This is especially effective for use in matching English and foreign language vocabulary words and even studying geography — state on one side, capital on the other.)

- Set information (such as the countries of Africa) to a song for more interesting, entertaining, and effective learning and review.

- Play "Memory" and other games which develop visual memory skills.

- Allow the child to invite a couple of friends over to study. Have each of the students make out ten questions he thinks the teacher will ask on the test. Then have the group take a practice quiz on the material — and grade each other's papers!

Visual Learning

Danny

Danny, a junior high student, finds that he does much better on tests when he makes out study cards early in the week, as soon as the new study material is assigned. For example, the molecule goes on one side of the card, its identification and picture on the other side. Danny goes over the cards first, and then carries them with him in his shirt pocket throughout the week. Several times a day during his spare time, he flips through and reviews the cards. By the time of Friday's test, he has mastered the material and feels confident.

He has found that color-coding the cards (using orange, yellow, and blue to distinguish different subjects) also aids him in his study.

An adult inmate

A prisoner in his thirties wanted desperately to learn to read. He had gone through all the grades of school and had received a diploma, but still his reading level was less than that of a third-grade student. A man who came to the prison regularly to tutor realized that this inmate's learning style was visual, that he had only been taught to read with phonetic methods. The tutor made up word cards with visual clues and accompanying materials, and the two men worked together weekly. For the first time in his life, the prisoner learned to read, slowly at first, and then more proficiently, because someone took the time to recognize and tap into his learning style.

Strategies for Promoting Visual Learning

It is important for the visual learner to develop good listening and communication skills and to learn to take good notes in order to stay tuned to lectures, class discussions, and other oral learning situations.

A student who has visual strengths but whose auditory memory is weak, may need an outline or chart or other visual accompaniment to keep up with oral presentations.

Looking at an outline or lecture notes while listening to the presentation greatly enhances his learning.

Following are some other ways to motivate the visual learner:

- Provide him with lots of slides, maps, diagrams, and charts.
- Give him opportunities to draw, paint, and build with a variety of materials.
- Use visual objects to represent abstract ideas or concepts. When he is learning geography, for example, a game like "Where in the World?" (which uses brightly colored shapes of countries), or a multi-colored map or puzzle, will help him relate the name of countries with specific colors or shapes.
- Buy flash cards and use make-your-own-study cards for any subject.
- Make use of the technique of "mapping" to motivate the writing of a personal experience story. First have the student draw a map of a camp area, grandmother's farm, or some other place which interests him. Then have him write down any story that comes to his mind while thinking about his favorite "fun place."
- Avoid disorganization. Visual learners are easily distracted by clutter: too many articles tacked on the board or too many changes in arrangement. It is hard for them to think and study in a disorderly environment. Encourage your child to clear away his desk and study area and keep study materials neat and straight.

The Combination Learner

Some children's strengths are a combination of two ways — visual/auditory or kinesthetic/visual learning, for example. The child who is strong in all three can shift strategies to fit the teacher's style, or learn information on her own (and may very well be labelled "gifted"). Maggie, one of my third grade students, was very verbal and communicative but also enjoyed drawing or reading for hours on her own. Since much of elementary instruction is visual and auditory, Maggie excelled and had many chances to shine in school.

Whatever your child's learning style, build on it and show her ways to use it and you'll help build confidence *and* her enjoyment of the learning process. (In HOMELIFE is a helpful quiz for parents to take to determine their child's learning style. Also see Dr. Wm. Barbe's excellent book *Growing Up Learning*.)

Encouraging Your Child's Talents

Kids can develop confidence and skills, and build momentum, in developing talent in drama and plays, in becoming an expert at fixing lawnmowers, playing the violin, baking, volleyball, diving, chess, ice skating, or working with computers. We never know where their interests and talents will lead.

Jeff Thompson, an Oklahoma teenager, began tinkering with the Apple computer his parents had given him when he was twelve years old, and discovered that he had a knack for technology. Through reading and hands-on experimentation he learned basic computer theories. At age fourteen, in his spare time, he founded Peripheral Outlet, a new and reconditioned computer sales and service firm (financed with money saved from his four-year newspaper route). Annual gross sales are now in the six-digit range.

In addition, Jeff enjoys playing trumpet in the high school band and taking part in leadership activities at school and church, while maintaining a 3.9 grade-point average.

All children's interests may not bloom as quicky and as profitably as Jeff's, but what matters is that the child has an opportunity to discover what he is good at and a chance to get the basic skills and encouragement he will need to make it over the long haul, because the process of developing talent takes time, patience, and enthusiasm.

Developing Goals

When a child has goals and aspirations, he is much more motivated to learn and can surmount obstacles along the journey to the realization of his objectives. If kids can relate their schooling with something they want to achieve in the real world, it can help fire their motivation. They can gain aspirations for the future by being around interesting people from various professions, through outings and part-time work, and by engaging in dialogue with parents and other adults in their community.

The candy-striper hospital volunteer may want to become a neo-natal nurse. The teenager who works in retail sales one summer may steer in the direction of marketing in college. Working with children at a summer camp gave Megan the desire to become an elementary teacher. Having become burned out with school in her sophomore year, life took on new excitement for one young lady when she got to be an assistant for a graphic artist on Saturdays.

When children are encouraged to think and talk about the myriad of opportunities there are in different fields of work, education can begin to make more sense to them. It fires their motivation, especially by middle school age, to begin to develop personal career goals.

How can we adults encourage their aspirations? Parents can introduce their children to their own vocation or profession so their youngsters can view first-hand what kind of work they do. Guest speakers from the community can spark school discussions and enliven career days. Some high schools give students a chance to work with and "shadow" a person in a profession in which they are interested. When writers, artists, and musicians share their craft and encourage children's talents in the classroom, enthusiasm can be ignited.

Physical therapist, landscape artist, homemaker, dolphin trainer, architect, journalist, scientist — today there are a tremendous number of opportunities for young people. As kids develop goals and aspirations for the future, their motivation is boosted.

Multiple Intelligences

As unique as fingerprints, individual learning styles are a key to greater motivation and achievement! We can also build on our children's strengths by recognizing their individual talents and gifts, in one area or in a combination of areas. "Gifted" children are not just those who score high on pencil and paper IQ tests. Every child has gifts and talents. As Dr. Howard Gardner, a Harvard University psychologist, has observed each child has one talent or a combination of talents he terms "multiple intelligences":[2]

- Linguistic intelligence
- Logical-mathematical intelligence
- Spatial intelligence
- Musical intelligence
- Bodily-kinesthetic intelligence
- Interpersonal intelligence
- Intrapersonal intelligence

Has your child been able to remember and repeat tunes from the time he was small? Does he play a musical instrument by ear? Does he have perfect pitch? If so, he probably has musical intelligence.

Is your child fascinated with word play? Has he been making up or writing down stories since kindergarten? If so, he may be linguistically gifted.

Spatially gifted children are great "drawers," as one of my second-graders once noted. They visualize naturally and love to make interesting designs and illustrations.

Bodily-kinesthetic skills show up on the athletic field, in dance programs, in sculpting classes, in mechanical and other "hands-on" endeavors.

Those gifted with interpersonal skills shine when they have a chance to work with other people. They tend to be natural leaders and communicators.

The child blessed with intrapersonal intelligence is reflective, aware of inner thoughts, and interested in independent study and research.

Talents + Interest + Success = Motivation!

Whether your child excels in singing, drawing, inventing, diving, math, writing, or woodworking — it is important to find his talents and gifts and encourage them by providing opportunities for them to blossom. This will help build the momentum he needs to learn in other areas.

A child's motivation often comes from being excited about something he has learned he does well or in which he has a great interest in knowing more about. Even a little success in his area of strength, talent, or interest provides a great boost to his motivation, as well as his sense of self-esteem and self-confidence.

Chapter 10

MOTIVATION BOOSTER #2:

DEVELOPING LANGUAGE SKILLS

When I was a little girl growing up as the fourth daughter of six in the Heath family, the dinner hour was a daily event I looked forward to: a noisy time of lively conversation, clattering dishes, and an occasional glass of spilled milk.

On Sundays the youngest of us, called endearingly "the Three Babies," sat around the kitchen table eating our roast beef and mashed potatoes, bending an ear to hear the delicious grown-up conversation in the dining room where Papa and Mama, Granddad and Grandmother, my three older sisters and a neighbor sat around the big lace-covered cherry table.

So on the other days of the week, sitting with the "big people" was such a treat, and perhaps the reason I relished the conversation — the ideas about candidates in an upcoming Dallas election (I thought "Barefoot Sanders" sounded like an interesting name for a mayor!), the news of the latest Nancy Drew book my older sister Diana was reading, plans about the next national bridge tournament my dad was going to play in.

The dinner table was where I was exposed to what was going on outside of my little world of paper dolls, "Mother, May I?" games, and persimmon mud pies. There I heard the neighborhood news, discovered what Mama found interesting in the daily newspaper, shared the condition of Blackie (our rabbit), and was informed about the wonders of South America which my sister Martha had brought home from school that day.

Literacy Begins at Home

"Research is now confirming that dialogue and collaboration form the foundations of moral and ethical development, critical thinking, judgmental maturity, and teaching effectiveness. Conversely, lack of dialogue and collaboration between the more mature and less mature threatens the bonds of closeness, trust, dignity, and respect that hold our society together."

H. Stephen Glenn[1]

Conversational skills are crucial to a child's later success in school and society. Children first learn to reason and express themselves by talking. But unfortunately, in a class of thirty students, out of every fifty minutes spent in school, each youngster gets to engage in open-ended talk only about forty seconds.[2] If children are "seen and not heard" (or worse, not seen at all) and denied time for adequate conversation, they will not be able to internalize language well enough to clarify, digest, or remember what they hear.

Research shows that the more proficient a child is in spoken language, the more successful she will be at reading written language. Motivated children tend to have solid language skills. The child who is a good listener can retell stories and repeat and follow directions. We know that good kindergarten and first-grade listeners and communicators become successful readers by the time they reach the third grade; good fifth-grade listeners do well on achievement tests in high school. And we also know that it is very difficult to teach reading comprehension skills to a poor listener.

But children don't become good listeners and speakers merely by engaging in listening and speaking in the classroom. If they are to develop good language foundations and abilities, they must do so at home; listening and speaking skills are a part of the valuable learning equipment they *bring to school with them*.

It has been proven that, even in the case of an eight- to eighteen-month-old baby, the amount of live language directed to a child in one-on-one conversation with an adult is vital to the development of basic linguistic and social skills. From the earliest years on throughout childhood, literacy development depends upon the amount and quality of language practice engaged in at home. These inter-personal skills enable the child to interact with teachers and other students at school, and, later, with employers and other important people in the outside world.

When communication lines between parent and child are open, learning and motivation are boosted. Dorothy Corkille Briggs notes: "Research indicates that children who do well on mental tests and in schoolwork are more likely to come from homes where there is a great deal of open communication. When parents and children are warmly interested in each other and their activities, when children feel safe to share ideas and feelings, intellectual growth is stimulated."[3]

Family Dinner Conversation

Although there are many places and times parents and children can talk together, one of the best ways to improve communication and boost language skill is to revive the tradition of the family dinner hour and to make it a priority in the home.

A family dinner hour in which a delicious meal and delightful conversation are shared together at the end of the day has the potential of becoming the centerpiece for each family member, from the youngest to the oldest, and of building family stability and continuity. Lively family discussion in a pleasant environment and setting builds a child's sense of self-esteem and develops her thinking skills and reasoning abilities. It provides her a time to reflect on the day's activities — her own and those of her parents and siblings.

One of the greatest aspects of family life is shared meals and conversation, says sociologist Robert Bellah, a professor at the University of California, Berkeley.[4] But because of a sharp increase in two-career and single-parent homes, and because of children's and teens' hectic schedules, the family that sits down together nightly for dinner and discussion is becoming more and more rare.

"The shared meal is really what you might call a family sacrament," says Bellah. "If you're going to have this sacrament, it means somebody's got to help mother — kids, husband — somebody has to help cook and clean up, and that should enrich meals as sacraments because everybody, not just one person, contributes."[5]

The question "What did you learn today?" has been a springboard for some interesting discussions at our house. We find that we can build relationships and enhance fellowship as we talk about goals and aspirations, friends and activities, and discuss interesting careers and people, sports, "school stuff," and current events. Bringing a newspaper or magazine clipping on a local, national, or international issue stimulates the free exchange of ideas. Sometimes Alison brings a poem she has just written to read to us, or a drawing she's completed to show us. Justin shares a debate on some important issue which took place in his ethics class. Chris tells us which teams are in the NCAA playoffs.

There is a great boost in motivation when parents can weave together what children are learning with other information and ideas, and when children and parents have open communication.

Two Families' Mealtimes

As a pre-teen one of my favorite books was *Cheaper by the Dozen,* an amusing and highly entertaining biographical account of the Gilbreath family written by one of the sons and daughters. I was fascinated with how Mr. and Mrs. Frank Gilbreath, both industrial engineers, ran their busy household of twelve children. Father didn't waste even a moment when the children could be learning, and both parents vigorously participated in learning programs of every conceivable kind.

In the Gilbreath home, a variety of educational projects were going on at all times throughout the house. There were frequent lectures, quizzes, and discussions. Everyone learned to type (even the preschoolers). French verbs and math formulas were posted on mirrors and closet doors, and French records played during dressing time.

The Gilbreaths didn't hold wooden, mechanical drills at mealtimes, but had lively games, challenges, and sharing as they ate. Maybe that's not quite your "cup of tea." (Your children might run from the table if you announced a quiz!) I'm not suggesting that we all imitate the Gilbreath household, but it did have one important ingredient that greatly motivated learning at the dinner table and in the family's shared life together: *enthusiastic parents who fully participated in the lives of their children and who were actively involved in their learning.*[6]

Leo Buscaglia, former professor, internationally known lecturer, and best-selling author, describes his family's "Dinner Table University":

"Papa believed that the greatest sin was to go to bed at night as ignorant as when we awakened . . . . To ensure that none of his children ever fell into the trap of complacency, Papa insisted that we learn at least one new thing each day. And dinner time seemed the perfect forum for sharing what we had learned that day. Naturally, as children, we thought this was crazy. There was no doubt, when we compared such parental concerns with those of other fathers, Papa was weird."[7]

Buscaglia goes on to describe how he and his siblings, while washing up for dinner, would ask each other, "What did *you* learn today?" They knew they would be asked to share the day's learning with Papa at the table. If the answer was, "Nothing," they wouldn't dare come to table without first finding a fact in their much-used encyclopedia. No dinner ended without each of the children sharing a new fact, whether it was the population of Nepal or the name of the highest mountain in Japan, while Papa and Mama patiently listened, responded, and perhaps found the place mentioned on the map. So during every dinnertime, with every sibling sharing what he or she had learned, they were enlightened by at least half a dozen new facts each day.

Although, as a child, he and his siblings would rather have been running off to join their friends in a game of "kick the can," Buscaglia says that, looking back, "I realize what a dynamic educational technique Papa was offering us. Without being aware of it, our family was growing together, sharing experiences, and participating in one another's education. And by looking at us, listening to us, respecting our input, affirming our value, giving us a sense of dignity, Papa was unquestionably our most influential teacher."[8]

Although his father, an immigrant from Italy, only got to attend school through the fifth grade before he had to go to work in a factory, his tremendous, enthusiastic motivation to learn was passed on to his son. As his Papa said, "How long we live is limited, but how much we learn is not. What we learn is what we are."[9]

Tips for Making Family Mealtime Count

Here are some tips to make your family's evening meal a time of learning as well as enjoyment:

- (Aim for a dinnertime that is agreeable with most of the family and that you can usually be consistent with.) It provides a sense of stability and security for a child to know, "We'll gather and eat at 6:30."

Then even if you're inconsistent for a week or so, you have a goal to "shoot for."

- Eliminate distractions like television (turn it off) and telephone (we unplug ours or take it off the hook during the mealtime).
- Have a centerpiece to focus everyone's attention in the center and brighten the table. It doesn't have to be fancy — a basket of miniature pumpkins or apples in fall, a jar of zinnias cut from the garden, or lighted candles.
- Avoid unpleasant or negative family business like hashing over report cards, nagging about problems, or handing out punishment for prior misbehavior.
- Encourage your children to become involved in the discussion, to participate, and speak up. Ask them questions and stir up their opinions. Make even younger members of the family feel a part of the conversation.
- Encourage listening, and not interrupting, respecting each other's ideas and opinions. Think of this hour as a time of encouragement and refreshment for everyone.

Roadblocks to Good Language Skill Development

In her excellent book, *Smart Kids With School Problems*, [10] Dr. Priscilla Vail points out factors that can hinder the developing language skills of children. They are in fact the unrecognized cause of many learning, behavior, and attention problems. Among these factors are day care, recurrent ear infections, weary parents, and the instant gratification of television and video.

We know that children develop vital listening and language skills through engaging in frequent conversation with adults. The problem is that the primary job of day care is to provide as much physical safety and security as possible, says Dr. Vail. In spite of good intentions, there are perhaps twenty to twenty-five (or more) children to each adult. So for a child like Jennifer, who has been in day care since the age of ten months, opportunities for one-to-one conversation and attention are very limited.[11]

This environment is in stark contrast to a reasonably warm home in which adult-child reponses, the key to education, will be *fifty to one hundred times more* than the average teacher-child response in day care or the classroom.[12]

In addition, in a day care setting a child like Jennifer has significantly more exposure to viruses, flu, and colds, which often develop into ear infections in small children. Research with thousands of youngsters shows that frequent middle-ear infections are a main cause of lowered acuity and perception and even some hearing loss. Jennifer may misunderstand directions, fail to experience vocabulary growth, and miss important foundations necessary for the full development of her intelligence. Yet these effects can go unnoticed until major learning gaps or problems surface.

Jennifer may come home to a weary mom who is so exhausted at the end of the day that talking and listening intently to her daughter's chatter may be extremely difficult. Instead of the desperately needed conversation between parent and child, Jennifer may get physical care, a nourishing meal, warm hugs, and perhaps a steady diet of evening television. Kids who become dependent on TV's qualities of instant gratification and vivid imagery may have trouble recalling, understanding, and processing their teachers' oral instructions.[13]

How can we overcome these roadblocks and help Jennifer and all our young children develop strong listening and language skills that will lay a solid foundation for their learning and motivation?

Suggestions for Developing
Good Listening Skills

Parents, in language, as in other areas, are a child's first teachers. By encouraging the development of listening skills, we usher our child into the wonderful world of language.

Besides encouraging dinner conversation, you can foster good listening habits, especially in younger children, by:

- Giving practice following directions.

- Even with young children you can begin with one simple request and then add to it: "Please bring Mom her boots." Next time: "Please bring Mom her boots, and close the door." And be sure to add: "Thanks! You're such a big help!"

- Playing games like "Simon Says" and "Command."

  In "Simon Says" the person playing Simon gives an order like: "Simon says, 'Pat your head.'" If the order is given with "Simon says," the players are supposed to do as instructed; without the phrase "Simon says," orders are not to be followed. Those who act without proper orders are counted "out." The last one correctly obeying Simon's orders is declared the winner.

  In "Command," children are given a list of things to do: "Pat your head, jump on one foot, and sing...." The winner is the one who follows the increasingly long orders without making a mistake.

- Playing all kinds of board games and engaging in word games to pass the time in the car as you travel together or at the doctor's office or other waiting times.

  The first player might say, "I'm going to Europe and will take an *apple* (or any other object beginning with the letter a)." The next player must repeat the sentence, adding an item that begins with the letter b. The game continues alphabetically, each player in turn repeating all the articles named before and adding his own at the end. A player is ruled "out" if she forgets an item, repeats items out of sequence, or supplies a wrong answer.

  Decide on a category (such as animals, living things, or places). If the category is animals, name one and have your child name another whose name begins with the last letter of the animal you mentioned. For example, you might say, "Goat." Then your child could say, "Tiger."

- Limiting television viewing.

  When you do watch a show on TV together, discuss it with your child. Ask cause-and-effect questions such as: "What do you think will happen now?" "Why do you think the main character acted like that?" Talk about what is real and unreal, true and false in television programs. If a particular show (such as a National Geographic special on whales) stirs your child's interest, provide him with some books on the subject.

- Reading aloud to your child!

  More about this later...in "Reading Through the Seasons."

- Listening to stories and poems on tapes and records.

  This is an especially good activity on short or long trips. Sing together as you ride along. Discuss the stories your child is listening to.

- Talking! Talking! Talking!

  Talk together with your child at home while digging in the garden; playing in the park; folding clothes; cooking; walking; eating breakfast, lunch, and dinner; driving to and from school; doing errands; and at bedtime (that special moment when the lights are out and a youngster will often share thoughts and feelings that have not come out all day!). Conversation about people, events, and things in the child's everyday life are vitally important links in language learning.

- Modeling good listening.

  This is the most important factor of all. When your child or someone else is speaking, be an attentive listener. Let your child know that you care enough, and are interested enough, to listen to what she has to say. Don't worry about correcting every mistake she makes because most errors will work themselves out as she grows and imitates good models of spoken and written English, both in conversation and in books.

  We all have a need to be listened to and understood. Sometimes children talk so much it takes a huge conscious effort and a firm decision to tune in with our eyes and ears to what they are saying — to listen actively. But such attentive listening is always worth the effort!

What's Black and White and Read All Over?

In our family, the daily newspaper has provided lots of informal opportunities for reading, talking, and listening. Sitting around the dining table one Sunday night, sandwich in hand, Justin finds an interesting sports quiz in the Sunday supplement and asks Chris, "Should artificial turf be phased out? Should athletes be subjected to random drug tests? Should the three-point shot in basketball be abolished?" Then follows a lively discussion between the two boys.

I share an interesting short article about the weather extremes in a New England April (the grayest and gloomiest in ninety-six years in Maine), and Alison reads us an article about Charles Dickens' first trip to Portland in the late 1800s.

It is unplanned and informal, but an interesting time together. We make comments and ask questions. Alison begins to work on her Caddie Woodlawn puppet for her social studies project. I start work on a magazine article. The boys continue to read the sports section and compare notes on the American League baseball predictions for the season ahead.

Inexpensive, spontaneous, and fun — here are some hints on how you and your family can use the daily newspaper to boost reading and writing skills:

- Sometimes one of us clips a cartoon and puts it on the refrigerator for everyone to read and enjoy.

- The classified ads are fun to work with. Each member of the family can pick out three jobs he would like to have one day in the future. He clips the ads and studies them, looking at the education, qualifications, and experience needed to land the position. Then he clips ads for three more jobs for which he already qualifies. Reading the want ads produces a lot of eye-opening reality!

- There's the weather section: what's it going to be like tomorrow, this weekend, next week?

- Clip interesting photographs from the newspaper and let your child write her own newspaper story.

- Matching game: cut out photos and captions. Then separate and mix them up. Your child can match the captions with the photographs.

- For a young child, cut up a comic strip and have him put it in the right sequence. For an older child, you can do the same ordering game by using paragraphs cut from an article of interest.

- Locate on your map or globe some of the places mentioned in lead stories of the day.

- Clip an article or editorial on a controversial local, national, or international issue and have a pro-con discussion of it at dinnertime.

- Make a "hero scrapbook." Save and share stories and articles on people in your community or state who have interesting jobs, are doing worthwhile things, or performing some special service for others. Also look for stories of people who have overcome obstacles or handicaps, or who have performed feats of courage or unselfishness.

Your child can collect these articles in a simple scrapbook. Children begin to develop aspirations and set goals as they are inspired by great acts of service or simple acts of kindness performed by unsung heroes they read about in the media.

- Ask your child to clip coupons from the food section of the paper. She can categorize and help redeem the coupons at the grocery store.

- Encourage your child and another friend to start a neighborhood newspaper. Each issue can include items on the arrival of new neighbors, a summer or fall trip, a "yard of the week," as well as letters to the editor, an advice column, and general news. It can even include ads for jobs or services needed or offered (like those of eligible babysitters), along with news of coming events like block parties or potluck suppers, and announcements of engagements, weddings, and new babies.

In Dallas, Texas, two boys, Ian and Barrett, aged eight and nine, wrote their own neighborhood newspaper and sold it for fifteen cents a copy. Besides learning how to run a business and get along with a partner, they also earned enough pocket money to collect baseball cards and plastic soldiers.

Reading Through the Seasons

What motivates a child to become an avid, lifelong reader? "Rainy days were special at our house," says Melanie Hemry, "and my love of reading began at home. My parents loved to read. When it rained on Saturdays and in the summer, we would all get up early, clean the house and get all the chores done. Then my parents, two sisters, baby brother and I would pile in the car and go to the library. Everyone would get to choose a book.

"When we got home Mom would make homemade doughnuts drizzled with icing. We'd curl up with our hot doughnuts and our books and read all afternoon.

"Whether at home or away, reading was a big and enjoyable part of our lives. On vacation, we'd go camping in Estes Park, Colorado. We'd fish, hike and stay busy all morning, but every afternoon there would be an hour or so of rain. We always packed a filled bookcase in the camping trailer. We'd scurry into the tent, light the lanterns, and lie on our cots and read with raindrops pelting on the tent. To this day, a storm cloud makes me automatically reach for a book. For us, reading was a family affair."

Every season brings a reason to share reading as a family, boosting your child's love of reading. Winter is a perfect time to enrich our children's education, encourage openness and conversation by reading aloud as a family. Reading aloud or silently by the fireplace produces wonderful memories. Reading while traveling, summer reading, magazine reading while recovering from a cold or flu, making library trips in spring and fall, reading recipes and cookbooks together while baking Christmas cookies — whatever the time or place, reading is a foundation for life. You can help your child become a better reader by your enthusiasm, your example, and your involvement in reading together.

Motivating Lifelong Readers
(Even Reluctant Ones)

You can motivate even reluctant readers by:

- Reading a child the beginning of an exciting book, and then asking her what she thinks will happen next. Most children will want to read the remainder of the book to find out what happens to the characters.

- Installing a clip-on light to your child's bed or placing a lamp on the bedside table, providing books in her favorite field of interest, and giving her fifteen to thirty minutes of time to read in bed nightly before lights out.

- Playing games that include reading, such as "Boggle," "Password," "Go to the Head of the Class," "Scrabble," and others.

- Letting your child subscribe to a children's magazine. In America, there are over 160 magazines for young people, and most of these periodicals can really help promote the habit of reading. These include nature tales, arts and crafts guides, history and science adventures. There are many fine publications that promote interaction with the child through high-interest articles, puzzles, games, letters to the editor, and pages for readers' writing, art, and other contributions. See your local library for a list and sample of helpful children's literature.

- Taking your child to a bookstore to spend her birthday or Christmas money on the purchase of a book by a favorite author.

- Allowing your child who is a slow reader, or who gets frustrated with books on her level, to choose a library book below her reading skill to read to a younger sibling.

- Dramatizing a story. After you read a book together, allow your child to dress as a character in the book and act out an event in the story.

- Using a computer, when possible, either at home or at the library or school. There are some excellent computer programs that promote interest in reading.

Two favorites of my friend Marilyn Phillips,* a reading specialist, are "Tiger Tales," and "Sticky Bears." In these programs, the child selects subjects and verbs from available choices, then the computer program produces the sentence in animated form. For instance, the child may choose, "The turtle chases the bear." Then she sees the sentence she has created come to life as it is acted out on the computer screen.

• Making use of large-print books like those published by Cornerstone Books.[14] These books are designed primarily for children ages eight to twelve and have received major awards for children's literature. They are produced in appealing, large-print editions designed to motivate reluctant readers or students with low vision or visual impairment that would make normal reading difficult.

• Finding a qualified person to evaluate your child and identify any problem areas in her reading development. Symptoms of problems include less than average work in school, delays in language development, and difficulty in memory, decoding, or comprehension.

Above all, let your child see your on-going enjoyment of reading for its own sake — novels, magazines, newspapers, or poetry. Your positive role-model as a reader is the most powerful motivation booster of all.

---

*My thanks to reading specialist Marilyn Phillips for her contributions to this section on ideas for reluctant readers.

Resources for Reading Development

There are some good resources for materials on your child's age and reading level and in his field of interest. These materials include age-graded recommendations of the best children's books, categorized into fiction, non-fiction, poetry, etc.:

- Jim Trelease, *The Read-Aloud Handbook*
- Judy Freeman, *Books Kids Will Sit Still For*
- Gladys Hunt, *Honey for a Child's Heart: The Imaginative Use of Books in Family Life*

You might also ask your librarian for a list of:

- The Sequoyah Children's Book award winners
- The Caldecott Medal children's books since 1938
- The Newbery Medal children's books since 1922

Chapter 11

MOTIVATION BOOSTER #3: STORYTELLING

> "We're a family and we're a tree
> Our roots go deep down in history,
> From my great-great granddaddy reaching
> up to me;
> We're a green and growing family tree."
> From "Family Tree"[1]
> by John Forster and Tom Chapin

During a family reunion, my husband and I, our children, and some cousins sat around Uncle John as he related a favorite Fuller story, "John Matthias Goes to Dodge City." Children and adults listened with wide eyes and attentive ears as Uncle John told tales of the Old West like this one:

"My dad, John Matthias Fuller, went to Dodge City, Kansas, as a young man before the railroad lines were built because Dodge was having a boom — lots of jobs, money, and opportunity. John was a city-slicker, but decided that since all the cowboys out there were wearing guns, and since he wanted to be in style, he'd go and buy a big six-shooter, belt and holster.

"One Sunday morning John thought he'd try it out and he sneaked down the street wearing his big shiny six-shooter (he was a peaceful man who'd never hurt anybody). Suddenly someone grabbed him by the collar and said, 'Hand me that gun and gunbelt.' That was Bat Masterson, the famous marshall of Dodge City. He said, 'Young man, you don't wear a gun in this man's town. You'll just be fodder for the guys who know how to use one. I'm going to take this gun and gunbelt and keep them in my office and when you leave, you can take them with you.'

"Well, Dad stayed there in Dodge City three months, and then he decided to go back to Kansas City to work for his older brother. Last thing he did was to go to get his gun. There was a clerk in the marshall's office who said, 'What will you take for that gun?' The clerk had a roll of bills and John had his receipt, so he sold the gun to him. So Dad didn't wear a gun very long, but he went to Kansas City a few dollars richer."

Throughout the afternoon, Uncle John spun yarns of the Fuller brothers staking a claim on the Cherokee Strip and told how John Matthias began his building career. He told us the story of "Grandma Fuller and Her Knitting Needles." During World War I all the townspeople brought her yarn and she knitted woolen hose and gloves for the soldier boys in France. Those little steel needles would fly while she read her big Bible propped up in front of her.

We all have a story to tell. Each family has a rich storehouse of tales: stories of faith and good character, stories of overcoming adversity, stories that show the frailties and mistakes of ordinary people. Bible stories provide the histories of men and women in the larger community of faith — David, Sarah, Ruth, Peter. We have stories of our nation's history — the Boston Tea Party, the Revolutionary War, the Underground Railroad of the pre-Civil War era — and stories about our favorite historical characters like Clara Barton or Paul Revere.

Have Our Children Lost Their Past?

> "A person without a story is a person with amnesia. A country without its story has ceased to exist."
>
> William J. Bausch

Cultural illiteracy has been added to the growing list of American students' academic deficiencies, in addition to a poor showing in math, science, reading, and writing. What is "cultural literacy" and why is it important?

Cultural literacy refers to a knowledge and understanding of the past and the present. It enables students to:

- Read more fluently and with greater understanding.

- Understand and appreciate the shared heritage, institutions, and values that draw people together as a nation.

- Gain new knowledge and put it into perspective.

C.S. Lewis, the famed Christian writer and philosopher, once suggested that in the heat of battle he would have more faith in a group of soldiers who knew the stories of their country — tales of the great heroes and leaders —

than in a group of soldiers who knew only their nation's constitution.

Unfortunately, recent research shows that American students do not know the history of their country, or even their own personal or family history. The average score of 7,800 high school juniors who were tested on their knowledge of history was fifty, an F. The majority didn't know when the American Civil War took place, or even the year in which Christopher Columbus discovered America.[2]

Our children, the survey concluded, have very little sense of the past.

Put the Story Back in History

When the story is taken out of history, as it often is when taught in a bland, textbook approach of merely pouring out fragmented facts and isolated dates, it lacks life and fails to motivate learning. But educational reformers have found that when the focus is placed on major events, the people who lived them, and the literature of the era in which the action took place, students learn and retain history much more readily.

One of my fondest memories of college life at Baylor University in Waco, Texas, is Mr. Reed's history class. On the walk over from the dormitory, my anticipation would begin to build. What tale of adventure, war, conflict, or danger would Mr. Reed spin today? I wondered.

"Don't you want to put on your swimsuit and sunbathe and watch soap operas with us instead of going to class?" my roommates tempted more than once, as I grabbed my books. I wouldn't think of missing class that day. Being in class and listening to Mr. Reed was much more interesting than watching television or a movie. Unlike many college history professors, he didn't drone on from old lecture notes; he made the characters, countries, and cultures come alive as he dramatized the historical events of the day through vibrant, exciting storytelling. I was "hooked on" history. It became my second academic major because I didn't want to miss a single thrilling episode in the unfolding saga of Western Civilization and American History.

Be a Storytelling Family

One of the best means of reversing the trend toward "cultural illiteracy" — recovering our past, passing on positive, enduring values to our children, and boosting their motivation for learning history — is storytelling.

In addition, storytelling provides incredible benefits for children's overall educational skill development: it instills good listening habits essential for school success, develops concentration and a longer attention span, helps children understand the principle of sequencing, builds comprehension, and expands vocabulary.

> "Storytelling can ignite the imaginations of children, giving them a taste of where books can take them. The excitement of storytelling can make reading and learning fun and can instill in children a sense of wonder about life and learning."
>
> What Works[3]

Besides these benefits, storytelling has great value for its own sake — the entertainment and sheer delight that a well-told story can bring to a child. A story is a love-gift from parent to child, grandparent to grandchild. Story-telling brings joy to a youngster. It also conveys a sense of security and family belonging (the child feels and knows, "I am a Heath," or, "I am a Morrison"), connecting the child to the past and giving him confidence to go on into an uncertain future. As Vance Packard, the American writer, once said, "Knowing, in a deep-down sense, where you are from contributes not only to your sense of identity but to your sense of continuity."[4]

Storytelling is a way to re-establish communication and closer contact between parents, children, and the extended family. Direct interaction is especially needed in an age when parents and children spend much more time watching television than in family conversation.

Storytelling helps develop a sense of compassion in children as they respond to and empathize with the distress and trials of others. It provides a bridge for sharing life and building relationships. Whether it is gathering around the family dinner table in the evening and telling the stories of each member's day at school, work, or play, or spending time together at a reunion relating bits of family history, storytelling provides a means of sharing in and passing on important life messages and creating precious family memories.

And what better way to relieve stress at the end of the day than a time of storytelling. The child relaxes in bed, the parent sits close by and reads or recites a favorite, oft-repeated tale. Slowly the bumps, bruises, and cares of the day fall away as the old familiar words soothe, comfort, reassure, restore. Then, just before "lights out," a moment of quiet prayer, and the child drifts off to sleep enfolded in God's safekeeping and the peaceful security of the home.

> "Storytelling is an act of devotion. When we read or tell a story with enthusiasm, we send children a clear message: I care so much for you that I want to give you the most precious gift I have — my time. During those moments, together, nothing but the story matters."
>
> Charles A. Smith

Spinning a Yarn

"Where do stories come from, does anybody know?

"Where do stories come from, and where do stories go?

"Stories come from deep inside, then they travel far and wide.

"That's where stories come from, that's where stories go."[5]

So say the words of a song by storyteller Marcia Lane.

But where do your stories come from? Your family has tales of past generations as well as stories of your own era: accounts of the struggles and hardships of the first family members to settle in this country, memories of what life was like for grandparents and great-grandparents when they were young, recitations of father or grandfather's experiences in the war, remembrances of your own childhood. There are also stories of your parents and their courtship and marriage, as well as your own marital history: your first meeting, your first home, your first infant. Youngsters love stories of their babyhood and childhood.

My own children never cease to delight in hearing me tell about how Justin climbed on the roof at age two, or the time Chris was investigating the mushrooms in a neighbor's yard and decided to grab a bunch and stuff them in his little mouth to taste, or when Alison took her very first ride in an airplane.

There are also religious stories to help children's faith grow: accounts of God's faithfulness and His working in the lives of the family members, histories of Bible characters, reviews of some of the parables of Jesus.

As a parent, you can tell favorite folk tales and original, made-up stories. Sometimes these stories just grow out of moments the parent and child spend together. My brother George has always spun a bedtime tale — "The Adventures of Cowboy Bob" — for his little boys, Zack and Jonathan.

How did the Cowboy Bob stories get started? In the family home hangs a painting of a cowboy on horseback herding cattle across a wide prairie. One day Zack looked at the picture and asked, "Daddy, what's that?"

"That's Cowboy Bob and his famous horse, Paint," answered George. That night he told the first of many Cowboy Bob stories. Cowboy Bob rides across the plains, he is chased by wild bush dogs and a herd of buffalo, he leaps across canyons and fords rivers. Cowboy Bob is a very active, adventurous "cowpoke" — because his creator has an active, fertile imagination.

Here are some valuable tips on parental storytelling from this veteran daddy/tale-teller:

- Use familiar story-lines. Children love repetitive themes and characters like the wild bush dogs or the herd of buffalo which are always chasing Cowboy Bob.

- Put the child into the story. For example, George says, "Cowboy Bob was riding by the ranch and saw Jonathan and Zack. He asked them to go fishing with him, and they caught the world's biggest fish!"

- Start the story and then let the child participate, complete the action. George says, "Suddenly Cowboy Bob came upon a...." He stops and asks Jonathan to tell what Cowboy Bob encountered (a rattlesnake). "He pulled out his trusty...." Again George stops. This time he lets Zack tell whether the object Cowboy Bob drew was a gun, a knife, a whip, or whatever. This type of active participation in the narration of the story holds the child's attention and encourages his creativity and imagination.

- Tell a story rather than read a book, if the child is very tired, because the lights can be extinguished or dimmed, allowing him to close his eyes and relax, thus quickly drifting off to sleep!

- Tell personal anecdotes. Most children (including George's boys) love to hear stories about when Dad and Mom were little. At Christmas they enjoy hearing about what toys Dad liked to get from Santa, or what kind of dolls Mom used to play with. In summer, they like to hear about parents' childhood summertime adventures and activities.

Storytelling Starters:
The Tale of the Mysterious Bear

My friend, Kay Bishop, operated a weekly carpool of first- through fourth-graders whose antics almost drove her crazy. So one October day, in self-defense (to keep the energetic riders quiet and to preserve her sanity), she started telling her youthful charges a made-up story entitled "The Mysterious Bear." From then on, every Wednesday, by popular demand, she added a new episode.

When they got into the car, the first thing the children would do was ask, "Will you tell us the rest of the bear story?" They would get very quiet and would be "all ears" as Kay continued the tale of the secretive bruin.

Kay's son, Nicholas, loved the stories so much he asked his mother to write them down so he wouldn't forget them. She agreed, on the condition that Nick would make up and write his own original episode about the bear, which motivated him to develop his writing skills.

Dr. James Dobson's beloved carpool stories about "Woof the Dog" resulted in his daughter Danae's writing a series of children's books.

More suggestions for story starters:

- *Instant tall-tales* can encourage creative storytelling. Name three unrelated objects for your child, such as a koala bear, an apple core, and a candle, or perhaps a giraffe, a haystack, and an Oreo cookie. Then have him make up a short three- or four-minute story using these objects in his narrative.

- *Round-robin tales* are good story-starters. One person begins the tale, the next person in the circle adds some more action and perhaps a new character, and then the story line passes to the next participant.

- *Begin collecting hats* for your child from garage sales, thrift shops, and Grandmother's attic. Hats stimulate dramatic play and serve as great story-starters.

- *Hold a "family story hour"* after dinner a few times a month (or when extended family gathers) in which anyone, including parents, may share a story. Invite a grandparent, friend, or neighbor to come and spin a yarn, recount a memory, or describe an adventure.

When are some other times the family can "swap tales"? Just about any time they choose. Storytelling doesn't just have to take place at the local library. For decades, librarians and folklorists have done us the great service of keeping the storytelling tradition alive and passing it on to future generations, but telling tales can be done at so many other times and in so many other places. That's part of the joy of storytelling — it's spontaneous; it can be engaged in while washing dishes, raking leaves, riding in the car, or waiting in the dentist's office. Dinner time is made even more enjoyable by an interesting account of the day's activities or by a rousing good tale or sentimental yarn.

Storytelling around the fireplace in winter or around a campfire during vacation is always a special treat. A starry night in summer is the perfect time to recount legends of the stars. In our family, a car trip provided an occasion for Holmes to tell "Sinbad stories" that made the time go faster.

Tips for Storytellers

At a storytelling workshop for teachers held at Oklahoma State University, I learned that storytellers are made, not born. That news gave me hope, and I breathed a sigh of relief. I *can* learn to be a storyteller, I thought. I can recover the lost art of spinning a yarn, and so can you! Although I had shared true adventures when I was growing up, I didn't consider myself a "natural-born" storyteller like my brother George, creator of the famous Cowboy Bob series. But I knew that there was a place to start.

Here are some things I learned which might help you become a better storyteller:

Learning a prepared story

To learn to relate a folk tale or anecdote taken from a book:

1. Choose a story you like. Read it over several times to make sure of your choice. If it is from a library book, you may want to photocopy it and save it in a special "storytelling folder." If the story is too long, you may need to condense it or delete unnecessary parts.

2. Begin to get an idea of the basic text. It is not necessary to memorize the entire narrative. Outline the main events in sequence, noting the primary characters and the important words. Review this outline mentally or on paper.

3. Try to picture the story by scenes.

4. Practice telling the story to the mirror or even to your pet — *in your own words.*

5. Record the story on tape, video, or paper. If you are a strong auditory/verbal learner, you might play back a copy of the story on tape a few times, perhaps while driving to work or doing some non-mental task. If you are a visual learner, you will be aided by re-reading the story or picturing it by scenes. If you are a kinesthetic learner, you will do best to type or write out the story.

6. When you practice, add your own gestures, dialect, repeated phrases, props (even a musical instrument), and use your own style to make the story yours.

7. Relax, be natural, and enjoy telling the story!

Generating a personal history story

To generate a personal history story, ask yourself (or a family member) these questions:*

---

*My thanks to storyteller Vivian Nida for these questions.

1. Can you picture your childhood home? (Try to picture it just as it was in detail or even draw a simple house plan of it: the yard, the tree you played under, the house, the fireplace or dinner table where your family gathered and think about events that happened there. You can even draw a simple sketch or plan of the house to jog your memory.)

2. Who were the people who lived there with you? (What were they like? Did you all get along well?)

3. What visitors came most frequently? (Relatives, friends, extended family?)

4. What kind of neighborhood was the house or apartment located in? (How did you feel about it?)

5. What was going on in the world at the time you lived there? (Who was President of the United States; was the nation at peace or at war; what was the economic and social climate like; which movies, songs, radio or television programs were popular; who were your favorite entertainers; what were the current fashions like)?

Thinking about these things usually generates many family stories.

Looking at old photo albums often "primes the story pump." Children love to look at baby pictures of themselves, siblings, and parents, as well as photos of relatives. They are often fascinated by the stories and history that surround these family images:

- "This picture of Aunt Earlene was taken in 1935 in Hollywood where she worked as a double for Dorothy Lamour in a Bob Hope movie."

- "This picture of Grandma and Granddad was made when he came back from the war."

- "This is a picture of your father and me on our honeymoon at Turner Falls."

To tell a true story from your own experience, *remember a specific age* (when you were eight years old, for example) and then share about the time during that period when you were happiest, saddest, or the most frightened. Relate the dialogue. Recall the sights, smells, tastes, sounds, and feelings of the experience.

Was there some special insight or discovery you gained from it?

Interviewing family members for stories

> "When an old man dies, a library burns to the ground."
>
> Old African saying

When the family gathers for a reunion, or when grandfather or a great-uncle come for a visit, that is a perfect opportunity for hearing and gathering stories. Have a cassette recorder and extra tapes on hand. Some families even video tape interviews for a lesson in living history.

Here are some questions to keep the stories rolling:*

- Where were you born?

- Who were the first family members to settle in this country? Why did they come and where did they settle? Do you know any stories they relayed or your grandparents told which conveyed what life was like for them or how they made their living?

- Can you tell me what life was like when you were young and growing up?

- Can you relate a story that was told to you as a child? What are some of your earliest memories? Adventures? Happy times or sad?

- What was school like for you? Did you have a favorite subject or teacher? Favorite games or pets?

- Who were your best friends and what did you do together?

- What was your happiest time in childhood?

- What beliefs or values do you think your parents tried to teach you to live by?

- Who influenced your life the most when you were growing up?

- What were your teenage years like? Courtship and marriage? Did you go to war?

- What have been the biggest problems, mistakes, or adversities in your life? How did you overcome them, and what did you learn from them?[6]

Children as Storytellers

In our storytelling group, Tammy told me about her Grandfather Maurice who, during the Great Depression, took a cow to college to pay for his expenses. Emily shared about her great-grandfather's mysterious forgotten sister. And Katie told of the time her mom accidentally drank kerosene from her brother's tent and had to have her stomach pumped!

The parents and teachers who share their love of storytelling will find their children storytellers too. You may

---

*These questions were excerpted from *How To Tape Instant Oral Biographies* by William Zimmerman, a wonderful resource for any family to have for taping family or personal history (see Note 5). Guarionex Press Ltd., 201 West 77th Street, New York, NY 10024.

catch your ten-year-old retelling a story you've shared with his little sister. Or your sixth-grader may decide to dress up as Martha Washington and tell the story of her life as an oral project for social studies class. Perhaps you have shared about the times you took a big first step (maybe you didn't succeed the first time, but you kept trying). Your child can also share his first big steps — memorable events like the day he rode his bike without training wheels or the first night he spent at camp away from home.

Besides enjoying the fun of a story well told, children who tell stories:

- Develop confidence in speaking in front of a group.
- Get practice expressing themselves.
- Learn to think on their feet.
- Become better readers and writers.

Your child may tell stories about friends, describe a trip to the circus or to visit Grandma, or relate a made-up fantasy. At such times, you need to be an attentive, interested listener, because what is important is the joy of the story shared, the warmth and closeness of the parent-child fellowship. It is not a time to be pressuring or hurrying.

Let's be storytelling families — beginning today!

Resources for Storytelling

- *Tell Me a Story: Stories for Your Grandchildren and the Art of Telling Them* by Charlie and Martha Shedd
- *Creative Storytelling* by Jack McGuire
- *How to Tell a Story* by Ruth Sawyer
- *The Way of the Storyteller* by Ruth Sawyer
- *Tales for Telling* by Katherine Williams Watson

- *Word Weaving: A Storytelling Workbook* by Catherine Horne
- *Storytelling: Art and Technique* by Augusta Baker and Ellin Greene

Chapter 12

MOTIVATION BOOSTER #4: ENCOURAGING A LIVELY CURIOSITY

When we moved to Yarmouth, Maine, and our daughter attended the intermediate school, a big change occurred. Each of the previous years in Alison's school career, science had been taught mainly from dry textbooks and consisted of memorizing facts, doing worksheets, and getting ready for tests, tests, and more tests. Much of science had remained abstract and downright boring for her. She had read the assigned material and studied for the exams, but was usually disappointed with the results. "I'm terrible in science," we had heard her say more than once, "I hate it."

So I took notice when Alison came home from her new school announcing at dinnertime, "Science is my favorite subject."

What's the difference? Why the great change? I wondered. I just couldn't wait to meet my daughter's new science teacher! Every day or so Alison came home excited about the flowers she and the other students had dissected, or the owl which had been brought to class, or the space shuttle project the class was going to work on. When I asked her why she was so enthusiastic about her science course, she replied: "Mr. Corbett doesn't just explain things once, assign us a worksheet, and expect us to memorize it for the test. He really cares about our understanding. He doesn't put me down for asking questions — in fact, he'll say, 'Good question, Alison.' And it seems like he wants us to enjoy science. When we were studying electricity, for example, we did experiments and had demonstrations every day."

Alison's grades showed as great an improvement as her attitude. This girl who had always felt sure that she was just not "science-oriented" (or, as she put it, "dumb in science") began making a hundred percent on almost all of her science tests!

America Is Getting an F in Science

"Chalk Up Another F: A Crisis Looms in Science," read recent headlines. The Educational Testing Service of Princeton, New Jersey, adds science to the growing list of subjects in which American students are weak. According to "The Science Report Card," a federally funded project, more than half of seventeen-year-old Americans are so poorly educated in science they can't perform basic technical functions. Even worse, the report stated, their knowledge of science is so limited they can't even benefit from special job training.[1]

Compared to students of similar ages in five foreign countries and four Canadian provinces, American thirteen-year-olds ranked last in math and near the bottom in science. U.S. ninth-graders didn't fare much better, ranking fourteenth out of the seventeen nationalities tested.

But even more alarming than their poor showing on test scores, the science deficit points to a shortage of students who will go into fields like the natural sciences, the medical professions, and engineering. By the year 2000, the U.S. will need between 450,000 and 750,000 more chemists, biologists, physicists, and engineers than it is expected to produce![2]

Science education is gradually undergoing change. There are schools in parts of the country that are doing a better job of teaching science by using "hands on" experiences to demonstrate and reinforce academic concepts like using a flashlight and ball to demonstrate heat and gravity, and dissecting tulips and carnations from wedding bouquets to study the reproductive parts of flowers, as Alison's class did.)

In one school, fifth-grade students watch as light beams bounce off mirrors, bend through prisms, and burst into rainbows. To study the effects of acid rain, other students collect pond, tap, and rain water and measure its acidity.[3]

Most American schools need to enliven science study to whet students' appetites for learning and to encourage, instead of dampen, curiosity.

Teacher training, laboratories, and equipment, and a new enthusiasm in science classes are all needed — especially in the early years, when students' attitudes about science are being formed. By the fourth or fifth grade, educators say, children decide if science is "for them" or not.

Then in the middle school and high school years, instead of just memorizing facts and doing worksheets in order to pass exams, youngsters need challenging experiments and projects to keep them interested and motivated. They also need role models from the community in science and technical fields who will come to the school and speak, share research information, and instill and inspire an interest in the vast field of scientific knowledge, experimentation, and discovery.

But in the meantime, while reforms are taking place, there is something else that is vitally needed: parent/teacher involvement. As parents we need to ask ourselves how we can spark our children's curiosity, ignite their interest in science, and answer their endless questions about the world about them. Children have lots of natural curiosity. Just how important is that curiosity in the learning process, and how can we stimulate it rather than squelch it?

Keeping Curiosity Alive

Curiosity is the desire for knowledge about something, an inquisitive interest, an eagerness for information. *Curiosity is a very important component of motivation, for when curiosity dies, motivation and enthusiasm for learning die.* Often asking why, really wanting to know the answer, is a characteristic of a gifted, bright child who is inquisitive about many things in life, from the nature of a tiny insect to how a car works. Girls can be as curious and interested in science as boys.

A curious child likes to work on special projects, try new ideas, and look for books that will expand her knowledge about the things which intrigue her. A curious child is like a little girl I know named Melissa who brings something new and interesting each week to her kindergarten "Show and Tell" time: some small animal bones found on a hike with her dad at a local nature center, a turtle shell, even a six-foot rattlesnake skin from the arid lands of southern Oklahoma! Melissa, like her dad, is an avid rock-hound and already, at age six, knows the name of each specimen. A curious child is like Jay or Carey, eight and ten years old, who have an insect collection they began as preschoolers. Fascinated with insects, they go to the library with their mom to look up information to identify each specimen before mounting it on a board they made for that purpose.

Curiosity is an ingredient that carries a child's learning far beyond the "3 Rs." So keeping curiosity alive is critical to motivation and the learning process.

Push, Pull, and Take Apart

Every normal child is born curious. As soon as they can, babies begin to explore their surroundings and take things apart (which is why we parents have to do so much "baby-proofing" to make our homes safe during the first few years of their young lives). As soon as they learn to crawl, youngsters start to investigate, experiment, and manipulate. Their favorite pastime seems to be getting into things — whether it's Mom's pots and pans or the kitchen knife drawer! Toddlers watch and imitate, discover and dismantle, "reach out and touch someone" — or grab something! They have an in-born obsession to find out how things work and why.

As soon as the little one can talk, she begins to ask questions, thousands of them. By the time she is three or four years old, she wonders about everything. "Why? Why? Why?"

"Why is the sky blue?"

"Why is the worm fuzzy?"

"Why is the snow cold?"

"Why does the cat have whiskers?"

This is a critical stage in the child's development and parents must be patient with her many "whys" and "how comes." Little children are driven by the need to figure out what everything is, how it works, and "what makes it tick." By the age of five or six most of them have developed basic attitudes not only about their world and the things in it, but more importantly about learning and the learning process. Most of the time these attitudes will have been formed and shaped by adults' responses to their questions and exploration during their early, formative years.

What Happens to Curiosity?

New research shows that by the time children are in junior high or high school, they don't ask much of anything any more. James Dillon, an associate professor of education at the University of California at Riverside, visited fifty-five social science classes in a Chicago high school to study the question-asking process. Not counting the usual "how long till lunch break?" and "how much longer till school's out?" *eight hundred students asked only eleven real questions which solicited learning information.*

Why the big change from early childhood insatiable inquisitiveness to later adolescent complete indifference? What happened to the question-asking? What are we adults doing to squelch curiosity — and thus children's natural motivation and enthusiasm for learning?

Dr. Dillon concluded that home is the best place for a child to learn to be inquisitive. Unfortunately he has found that parents don't always encourage question-asking. In fact, often parents and teachers get irritated with the many questions youngsters ask.

Children's questions are important for information-getting, but also as expressions of their budding sense of initiative, says Dr. David Elkind. If we adults respond appropriately and positively to their questions, we provide youngsters with a feeling that the effort involved in *taking the initiative to ask* is worthwhile. We thus provide them with the important foundation they need in order to take initiative as older children and adults.[4] *And having the confidence to take initiative is a vital part of motivation for learning.*

Also, children need to be assured that if they are curious about something and there is no one around to answer their questions, they can learn to use the resource materials available to find answers for themselves.

But if we adults ignore the importance of children's questions, we lose not only an opportunity to encourage their initiative, Elkind says, we also contribute to their associating curiosity with a sense of guilt.

What happens when we are put off by children's questions and discourage their experimentation and discovery? If Holly's curiosity is rejected when she reaches for a roly-poly on the sidewalk or wants to stop and watch a bird and ask why it can fly, if her parents are irritated by her exploration and inquisitiveness, then she will get the message that it is not safe to ask or learn because it only gets her into trouble. "Don't touch that! Be quiet and come on!" When she is quiet, still, and passive, her parents approve and make her feel that she is a "good girl"; when she is inquisitive and curious about the world around her, she is a "bad girl." What is Holly being taught? *Not to learn!*

"Questioning and experimentation with the unknown form the basis of advance in every field," says Dorothy Corkille Briggs. "Stamp out these qualities that are present in every normal newborn child to some degree, and you literally hold back progress for the human race. Every parent and teacher is responsible for keeping the lights of curiosity burning in children. Every child must know that it pays to wonder. He must think no less of himself because of his push to know."[5]

A parent's attitude of actively encouraging questions and positively responding to his child's wondering and exploring goes a long way toward keeping curiosity alive. On the road to knowledge, parental attitude can be a STOP sign (which orders the child not to ask, touch, try out, explore or learn!) or a GO sign (which gives her the "right of way" to keep traveling toward her destination).

A homelife transfused with a "let's think and talk about this" atmosphere is a great foundation for lifelong curiosity and learning.

Handling Questions

As parents, at the end of our day we are often at the end of our rope — too tired and too busy with personal and family concerns to give full attention to a child who asks a question, especially a whole string of questions. It is hard to always be attentive and encourage children's curiosity. But the overall pattern of *how* we handle their questions (hopefully with patience, attentiveness, and interest) is important. It is helpful to a child to have an atmosphere at home in which she feels comfortable raising, discussing, and thinking through questions aloud with family members.

You might answer a question as simply as you can with as much detail as possible in the time available. In some instances (as when pressed for time), your answer as to why the grass is green may be, "Mommy doesn't know, but maybe one of our books can tell us," or, "That's a really interesting question; let me think and we'll talk about it at the table in a few minutes."

Dr. Jess Smith, father of four busy preschoolers and an award-winning science teacher, says that if he or his wife can't answer a question from one of their children, they say: "Daddy (or Mommy) is busy right this minute, but later we'll go to the library and look it up."

If you have a reasonably good home library with a good set of encyclopedias and access to the public library, you can consult one or the other to find the information you need to answer just about any question.

Here are some suggestions on handling children's questions:

- Try to answer your child's questions as thoroughly as possible within the time you have; but unless the youngster is asking for details, try to avoid using technical language.

- Give the child time to explain what she already knows and what she wants to know about the subject. Try to discover what she is really thinking at her current level of reasoning. You can build on what your child already knows or jog her memory by saying, "Remember what we said last week when we talked about this question?"

- Help your child think through the question and deduce possible solutions. In some cases, the child just sees something which sparks her curiosity. Without giving it any real thought, she immediately turns around and seeks a ready-made answer from the nearest adult. She probably has an idea or a clue to the answer, but just hasn't taken time to think it through. As parents, we don't have to feel that we must give our children all the answers they seek. Instead we can help them think through their questions and guide them in discovering the answers by asking them questions in return: "Why do you think?" Sometimes, children can come up with some interesting theories, and can formulate answers pretty well, says Dr. Smith. In science we call such a theory a "hypothesis" and encourage children to form and test their own.

• Give your child a sense that you are also curious and interested in how and why things work in the world around you.

Turn About Is Fair Play

When the Smith family goes to the zoo, they ask their children questions to get *them* to thinking:

"What does this animal eat?"

"Why does this animal have long legs?"

"Is this animal a meat-eater or a grass-eater?"

"Why is this animal's coat so thick and white?"

In our zoo there is an Indian elephant and an African elephant in the same pen. Dad might ask, "How can you tell the two different types apart?" and suggest that the children look at the elephants' ears. The family can also play a version of the "Sesame Street" song that goes, "Which one of these is not like the others?"

We can encourage children to let their minds go a little by asking them, "What would happen if...?" Sometimes we can nudge them to use their imaginations by asking, "What can we do with this tin can?" Or we can motivate them to "brainstorm" by asking, "What are all the ways we can use a toothpick?" They can wonder and think creatively about questions like, "What can we do with this styrofoam tray?" (Answer: "We can make an airplane out of it, or grow seeds in it, or....")

The questioning process hopefully will continue all through children's growing-up years. "For middle school and high school students, we need to be careful not to 'put them down' for their different answers," says Dr. Smith. "In a classroom, teens are more peer-conscious than adults, and giving wrong answers causes them to 'lose face.' This fear of 'looking dumb' because of an answer can do much to stifle youngsters' inquisitiveness."

But one way we parents can help our children is by never "putting them down" for asking questions or offering less-than-brilliant answers. We can remember that there is no such thing as a stupid question — only ones perhaps that have not been carefully thought through. We can ask thought-provoking questions while at the dinner table or when riding together in the car. We can ask for our children's opinions and theories, and be supportive when there is a hobby or interest they want to pursue. Reading science magazines and clipping newspaper articles on a subject like funding the local zoo, or discussing a conservation, health, or environmental issue can also stimulate questions for our teenagers.

If we give children opportunities to inquire and explore, if we encourage their questioning, they will continue to observe, wonder, make speculations, and connections throughout life. As John Holt said in his excellent book, *Learning All the Time*, "the process by which children turn experiences into knowledge is exactly the same, point by point, as the process by which those whom we call research scientists make scientific knowledge."[6]

Exploring Within Limits

Little children need safe surroundings at home in which to explore and play. They need a sanctuary where they can be free to use their eyes, ears, fingers, and noses to find out more about things, to investigate and discover. They need a place for times to explore within limits, because they learn through direct, first-hand experience with the people and objects in the world around them. And they need the safety of limits and supervision, because their curiosity can lead them into danger — like the time I mentioned during one of our "nature walks" around the block when our toddler stuffed his mouth with some poisonous-looking mushrooms which had sprouted in a neighbor's yard.

Using all of their senses, children begin to form ideas about how things work and start to make sense of their surroundings. They develop security and confidence as they wonder, discover, and gain knowledge for themselves. All this concrete learning is a vital foundation for later abstract, symbolic (pencil and paper) learning in books and school.

Children need a variety of experiences inside and out, at home and in the community. If we live in the city, we can take our youngsters to visit the zoo or a ranch or farm. If we live in the country, we can plan a little excursion downtown, perhaps riding the bus, taking a walk down a busy street, riding an elevator or escalator, going to a bank. Blair Redfearn, a geologist and father, takes his daughters on hikes at a local nature center. There they observe deer tracks, watch snakes eat fish, feed the perch, and learn about different kinds of trees. When out in the country, they stop by a field and watch a flock of turkeys. In the city they go to a pet store to look at colorful parrots and snakes and a great variety of fish and small animals.

Other places children can visit and learn are: an airport, a construction site, a bakery, factory, museum, planetarium, park, television weather station, or lumber yard. One dad I know took his children to a greenhouse and plant nursery. They watched the potting and repotting of plants and saw different varieties of flowers, plants, and trees. They learned how the nurseryman controls pests and how he controls plant diseases. They went home and planted seedlings in paper cups and egg cartons to make their own indoor garden.

Gordon Corbett took his daughters to a nearby city's flowering rose gardens, not just to rush through and glance at the beautiful blossoms, but to carefully observe and become familiar with the different varieties of roses: "We got close enough with a magnifying glass to look inside the flowers. It's so easy to carry a small magnifying glass; I always keep one in my pocket. We looked at all the different colors and sizes of hybrid roses."

We tend to think that if our children aren't busily doing something "constructive," they aren't learning, but often quiet reflective times lead to their stopping and thinking about the "whys."

Many years ago, Dr. Arnold Gesell suggested an ideal place for children to learn:

"Lead your child into nature. Teach him on the hilltops and in the valleys; there he will listen better. But in these hours of freedom let him be taught by nature rather than by you. Let him fully realize that she is the real teacher, and that you with your art do nothing more than to walk quietly by his side. Should a bird sing, or an insect hum on a leaf, at once stop your talk. Birds and insects are teaching him."[7]

Chapter 13

MOTIVATION BOOSTER #5: AWAKENING THE POWER OF OBSERVATION

Nature is a wonderful teacher. During anthropologist Dr. Margaret Mead's early years growing up on a farm, her grandmother sent her into the woods and fields to collect samples of wild plants. Then she showed her granddaughter how to closely observe and distinguish between various kinds of wild flowers, plants, and animals. As she grew to be an adult, Dr. Mead devoted her life's work to discovering and researching how peoples' lives are affected by their environment. Mead felt that the success of her whole career was built upon the sharp observation skills she had gained as a child. She had learned early the wonderful power of observation.

One of the foundational principles of science is observation — paying careful attention, being alert, and discovering things that would not have been noticed in a brief glance. Two very simple tools can aid a child's budding observation skills, stir up his curiosity, and focus his concentration — a magnifying glass and a paper towel roll to look through.

Mr. Corbett, our favorite science teacher, gives each of his sixth-grade students a paper tube and says, "Okay, we're going out today and look at the grass." The children reply: "What do you mean? We've seen grass before." "I know," answers Mr. Corbett, "but you haven't seen it very closely."

Just as we often can't see the forest for the trees, many times we can't see the grass and observe the tiny creatures and growing things in it because there are so many green blades in the way! We don't really stop and look. The paper towel tube limits and focuses children's vision so they can concentrate and see things they have never noticed before.

"I've had kids get down on their hands and knees with their tubes, and all of a sudden I hear, 'Oh, my goodness, come here, come here!' " reports Mr. Corbett. "And I find myself being pulled in four or five different directions. One youngster finds a hole, and in that hole is a worm or insect, and they all say, 'Oh, that's gross!' Another sees something else, little piles of dirt being thrown around by a beetle digging down through the soil. Another sees little spiders he never knew existed. The children see tiny flowers, Queen Anne's lace." It's amazing all you can see when you really concentrate on a small area.

The magnifying glass also comes in handy for observing in more detail. When you and your child are near a flower garden, you can say, "Have you ever really looked inside a flower?" Then you can give a little gasp as you observe with your magnifying glass, and your child will become curious. (As we have seen, a parent's enthusiasm is a key motivator.) The child will want a chance to look and see what is inside that bud. Then you can take one or two of the flowers (tulips work well), lay them out on a piece of dark paper, and give the child a pair of scissors. He can cut the flowers and see the pollen which shows up clearly against the dark background. Together you can look at and identify the parts of the flower. In this way, your child gets to do a little basic botanical investigation, and, best of all, his curiosity is aroused. You can also use the magnifying glass to more closely observe leaves, tree bark, skin, hair, fingernails, and objects around the house.

As you observe, you can find books for your child to use to find answers to his questions and to expand his growing knowledge and interest. You can go out on a field trip together and collect wildflowers, and then get a little pamphlet or booklet to help identify those you have collected. (Handbooks on different types of birds, flowers, shells, and stars are great — easy to read, but not too simple for the older child or adult who wants a basic primer in nature.)*

Nature Walks

Blair Redfearn used to take his six-year-old daughter Melissa on nature walks and point out the difference between a spider and an insect (eight legs versus six legs). In fact, that's the way Melissa learned to count; wherever she went, she checked out the local "bug population."

Blair had collected rocks from the time he was a child. He also collected small animal bones which he reassembled with glue to recreate the animal's skeleton. "If you're doing interesting things yourself," he points out, "your children become curious and ask questions." His daughters join him

---

*See the list at the end of this chapter.

as he polishes rocks in the garage or does his woodworking projects.

Now Melissa has her own rock collection with agates, fossils, aquamarine and others, a collection of small animal bones she found under an owl's nest, and the most interesting assortment of "Show and Tell" material imaginable, including a porcupine head! She has learned to enjoy observing her surroundings wherever she goes.

Keep a backpack or tote ready for exploring or short expeditions. In it, you can include:

- A magnifying glass
- An empty paper towel roll for observing (it can be cut in half for a more convenient size for smaller youngsters)
- A "critter jar" (a glass or plastic container fitted with a mesh lid to let in air)
- Old plastic tubs with snap tops for storing "treasures" found along the way
- A sturdy old spoon for digging

Collections

Collections are a great way to encourage a love of science and the development of observation skills. Children can collect shells, leaves, insects, or anything which interests them. Some youngsters like to collect baseball cards, stamps, and spoons from different places. All they need is a shelf, drawer, or shoe box for display and storage. Organizing and arranging their collection lays the groundwork for the intellectual skills of classifying, categorizing, and evaluating.

Stargazing and Storytelling

"Oh, look at the Big Dipper up there. Wow, there's the outline of a huge giant in the sky. And there's 'beetlejuice' (Betelgeuse or Betelgeux, a variable red star of the first magnitude, located in the constellation Orion); do you know that its temperature is 3,500 degrees?" When scientific facts are tied together with mythological stories, stargazing takes on a whole new meaning for children.

To early stargazers, Orion, a bright constellation seen in the eastern sky during fall and winter, resembles a hunter. Ancient peoples saw all kinds of figures in the starry skies and made up interesting tales and myths about them. Weaving these stories from mythology as you lie out in the grass on a blanket watching the stars can be great backyard astronomy. Storytelling is one of the "tricks of the trade" in capturing children's interest in science, says Gordon Corbett. An open space free of the interference of house or street lights is best. If you can get a star map from a planetarium, college, or science museum, or a book on astronomy from the local library, you'll be off to a great start.

Hamsters Anyone?

Having pets at home gives children a daily chance to observe the habits and activities of animals. Even infants and toddlers love watching fish in an aquarium. Dr. Jess Smith says that their child enjoys a parakeet, a dog, and enough fish to fill two aquariums. Rabbits, gerbils, and kittens are favorite childhood pets. One little friend raised white mice. We went through the hamster phase of our life and are glad to be safely back to a nice Sheltie dog, "Lady," for our family pet. When children are old enough, taking care of pets builds a sense of responsibility and dependability.

A Nature Scavenger Hunt

Scavenger hunts are a lot of fun for children and a good way to teach them to collect various types of interesting specimens. For an interesting afternoon, try taking several youngsters on a nature scavenger hunt. In a park, nature center, or forest give each child a variety of things to look for. The objects can be divided into lists and the children into competitive teams, or the youngsters can hunt in pairs for nature items such as:

- 5 different kinds of leaves
- 3 varieties of wildflowers
- 3 different pine cones
- 4 specimens of rocks

A good art activity after a nature hunt is to create a texture design on heavy construction paper. Your child can make an interesting nature print by dipping objects such as sticks, nuts, shells, leaves, and wood scraps found on the scavenger hunt into ink, tempera or acrylic paint.

A Seaside Scavenger Hunt

A great way to whet your child's curiosity and interest in science and to sharpen his powers of observation is with some "hands on" oceanography exploration — the seaside scavenger hunt. When I went on a beach scavenger hunt with ten-year-old girls, I learned more about sea creatures in one day than I ever had in years of textbook science classes.

This activity is best engaged in at low tide. Each person or team will need a small bucket, or a plastic container with a snap top, and a net or sieve. The "finds" expected of the children can be geared to their age levels. It may be best to pair an older child with a younger member of the family.

You can list (and cut out or draw a picture of each item for younger children): sand dollars, hermit crabs, Irish moss and sea lettuce, different kinds of snails, sea urchins, slipper shells, blue mussels, crabs, clam shells, driftwood, starfish, sea gull feathers, horseshoe crabs, lobster tails or claws.

It helps to wear rubber boots or tennis shoes so you won't slip on the wet rocks, and it's good to carry a stick along to use to pry a sea urchin or starfish from a rock (instead of using your hands). After the hunt, a small prize can be given to the person or team who has found the most items or carried out the most instructions, or the occasion can be celebrated with a picnic and treats for everyone.

After our seaside scavenger hunt at Cape Elizabeth, Maine, we picnicked on the huge granite rocks which provided us a lovely view of Casco Bay and the lobster boats at work. The sun quickly was replaced by the thick fog that rolled in, but the change in weather didn't dampen our spirits. Our seaside scavenger hunt was a great way to combine learning with lots of fun at the beach.*

A Potpourri of Home Projects

Chemistry sets, microscopes, and electronic sets are great, but you don't need special equipment to have some science adventure right in your own kitchen or backyard. Here is a potpourri of simple projects you and your child can do at home. But remember to follow your child's lead and interests and don't force these ideas:

- Make a birdhouse or feeder for the backyard. Even a claypot tray with sunflower seeds will attract an

---

*My thanks to Yarmouth Intermediate School where I was invited to go on my first seaside hunt.

interesting population of feathered friends to watch and identify.

- "Adopt" a local tree. Your child can collect its leaves in each season; note seasonal changes in foliage, size, and color; and record in a log book the different amounts of water the tree needs at various times of the year.

- Learn to use a compass. Hide a "treasure" in the back yard or a park. Make your child a treasure map using several simple directions: "Go SOUTH five steps. Walk WEST three steps. Walk NORTH six steps. Turn EAST ten steps. There's the treasure!" After you show the child where to start, he can use the compass to search for the hidden treasure. At the same time he will be learning to use a basic piece of scientific equipment.

- Set up a weather station in the backyard (your local library has good books telling how) or encourage your child to observe the weather and record his observations on a homemade weather calendar. Each day have him note whether it is cold, hot, rainy, windy, humid, stormy, etc. Put up an outdoor thermometer you can both see to check the temperature on a daily basis.

- Prepare a vegetable or flower garden. There is lots of science to learn in growing things. Your child can have his own little patch of ground in the backyard. Or you can take half of a wooden barrel, fill it full of potting soil and manure, or commercial fertilizer and lime, and let the child grow whatever he wants to — vegetables (even potatoes) or flowers. Seedlings can be started inside and then transplanted outside when weather permits in late winter or early spring.

Then your child can water and weed his own little "garden" (thus learning to distinguish a weed from a good plant), and eventually enjoy the fruits of his labor.

- Collect and save autumn leaves in wax paper pressed with a warm iron or between two sheets of clear contact paper.

Kitchen Science

Mr. Corbett's favorite saying, the one he lives by and practices in teaching children, is:

I hear and I forget.

I see and I remember.

I do and I understand.

There are lots of simple experiments we can do in the kitchen that help children develop the basic skills of asking questions, making observations, coming up with some sort of hypothesis to explain the phenomenon, testing their theory, and drawing conclusions.

While doing these kitchen experiments, consider asking questions to encourage your child to:

- Compare: "How are these two substances different?"
- Predict: "What would happen if...?"
- Observe: "What does this look (smell, taste, feel) like?"
- Consider cause and effect: "What happens if we do this (or don't do that)?"

Here are some ideas to get you started:

- Bobbing Coffee Grounds Demonstration: Instead of throwing away your old coffee grounds, use them for an experiment. Take a teaspoonful of them and pour them into a glass of ginger ale. They will sink until they collect enough carbon dioxide from the carbonated water (the tiny bubbles are microscopic so they can't be seen with the naked eye). The coffee grounds will now float to the top of the glass, release their bubbles, and then sink again. If you get 400-500 coffee grounds bobbing up and down in a glass, your youngster will want to know, "Why is that happening, Mom?"

- Colored Water and Oil Experiment: Take half a jar of food-colored water and half a jar of oil. Cap off the contents and you have a miniature ocean in a bottle. The water, which is heavy, will sink to the bottom, while the lighter oil will float on top. Tip the bottle back and forth and you will set off a wave action inside. You can ask the child, "Why don't the oil and water mix?"

- Egg Mysteries: To demonstrate buoyancy, put a pint of tap water in two jars. Add eight tablespoons of salt to one jar and mix. Then put an egg in each jar. Your child can watch as one sinks and one floats. If the child seems interested, you can ask him to speculate as to why an egg will float in salt water but not in fresh water. You can talk about what makes the difference.

- Balloon Fun: Get a handful of different-sized and various-shaped balloons. Blow them up and let them go one at a time. Let your child make some observations: how far each goes, whether the flight was straight or erratic, how long each stayed in the air, etc. You can ask, "Why did this big one not go as far as the little one?"

Have the child take the same balloons and tape a straw onto each one, blow it up again, run a string through the straw, stretch the string all the way across the room and let the balloon go. Swish! The balloon will shoot across the room because it has a guidance system!

These activities teach the child about mass and velocity while giving him a chance to have a lot of fun with balloons.

- Bubble-Blowing Activity: With bubbles you can demonstrate viscosity, i.e. how the molecules stick together in the sphere. It takes about one-quarter cup of dishwashing liquid and three-quarters cup of water to make good bubbles. For longer lasting bubbles, add a teaspoon or two of glycerine. If the child gets his hands wet, he can hold the bubbles he blows; if he touches them with his dry hands, they will usually pop. Ask him why. With a pair of rubber gloves he can handle the bubbles and build them into pairs.

- Cooking Questions to Ask Your Child:

    1. "Why does bread rise?" (You can talk about the yeast growing.)

    2. "Why should we be careful to wash our hands before we prepare food?" (Good starter for a discussion of microbes and germs.)

    3. "How can you tell from the bedroom when I'm fixing pizza?"

The key to the success of all these kitchen and backyard science adventures is the enthusiasm shown by you and your child. If you show interest, it's likely your child will also enjoy the observation or experiment.

> "Childhood's learning is made up of moments."
>
> Eudora Welty
> *One Writer's Beginnings*[1]

Having an attitude of spontaneity is important. If it rains, you can walk together with your child under an umbrella, splashing through the puddles and talking about what causes it to rain. If it thunders and threatens lightning, it is best to take shelter — then you can show your child how to determine how far away the storm is. (As soon as you see lightning, start counting the seconds until you hear thunder; that number divided by five tells you how many miles away the center of the storm is from where you are.)

Keeping a sense of wonder and discovery about the marvelous world around us is a powerful motivator for a child's lifelong love of science.

Tips for Science Fair Projects

Once a year at most schools, it's science fair time! This time can be enjoyable for parents and children, or it can be a real trial, depending on the preparation and attitude. If children have some of the "hands on" opportunities described in this chapter provided for them at home and at school, they may begin developing an area of interest which they would like to explore and experiment with as a project. We can give children things to manipulate and try to figure out. They can then build on what they learn, perhaps culminating with a journal or log of what they did and observed.

When your child is assigned a science fair project to decide upon and present, here are some ways to help him get started:

- Brainstorm ideas together
- Consult science books at the library
- Check encyclopedias on topics your child is interested in
- Read together about the topic and note what sparks his interest
- Watch "Mr. Wizard," "3-2-1 Contact," or other such children's science shows on public TV
- Visit science museums in your area

Remember to treat the project as a learning experience for your child, not as a display (for which you provide the majority of the thought and work) done just to impress the judges. In the long run, it hurts the child's learning possibilities and chances to do well in the fair if it is the parent's lettering and art work being presented. Judges interview children (not the parents) about their entries, asking them how the exhibit works.

Hands-on experiments that the child has done with even simple resources impress judges. For example, a student grows a group of bean plants with various degrees of light, demonstrating the results produced by each amount; nothing spectacular or "showy," but very effective and educational.

What is important is that your child is interested in and enthusiastic about his project. The teacher will check the project beforehand and hopefully help the child not to get too elaborate or beyond his ability. For parents, it helps to have the child make up a list of supplies he will need for the project — far ahead of time, not the night before the work is due. (The closer to the deadline the project is undertaken and the more pressing the time becomes, the more parents feel compelled to get personally involved in the actual planning, constructing, and displaying.) Instead of taking over, we can supply materials, encouragement, interest, counsel, and discussion for the child who does the project himself — with us as his cheerleaders!

Science Resources

There are wonderful books on all aspects of science — from saber-toothed tigers, lasers, and oceanography to volcanos, earthquakes, butterflies and whipporwills — to encourage your child's curiosity and enliven his interests. Here are a few for sharing with your kids from the public library, and ones that make good resources for your home library.

By Seymour Simon:

- *101 Hidden Questions = Answers about Dangerous Animals*
- *Hidden Worlds*
- *Jupiter, Saturn, Mars*

By Millicent E. Selsam:

- *A First Look at Flowers*
- *The First Book of Sharks*

By Ruth Heller:

- *How to Hide a Butterfly*
- *How to Hide a Polar Bear*
- *How to Hide a Grey Treefrog and other Amphibians*

By Patricia Lauber:

- *Volcano*

By Hedda Nussbaum:
- *Plants Do Amazing Things*

By Lenora and Arthur Hornblow:
- *Animals Do the Strangest Things*
- *Insects Do the Strangest Things*
- *Birds Do the Strangest Things*
- *Fish Do the Strangest Things*

New True Books by Children's Press:
- *Experiments with Light*
- *Experiments in Sound*
- *Weather Experiments*

National Geographic series of science books, such as:
- *Hidden Worlds*
- *Why in the World?*

By Rose Wyler:
- *Science Fun with Peanuts and Popcorn*

Golden Guides from Golden Press:
- *Flowers*
- *Trees*
- *Non-Flowering Plants*
- *Seashores*
- *Zoology*
- *Zoo Animals*
- *Insects*
- *Spiders*
- *Seashells*
- *Amphibians*
- *Reptiles*

- *Fishes*

By Susan Milord:

- *The Kids' Nature Book: 365 Indoor-Outdoor Activities and Experiences*

Chapter 14

MOTIVATION BOOSTER #6: WHERE IN THE WORLD IS NAIROBI? (ENCOURAGING KIDS TO LOVE GEOGRAPHY)

We waited in the high school parking lot on a cold November Maine evening with other families who, like us, would be hosts for a week of an international student from "Up With People." Soon buses pulled in and young people from all over the world began filing off, excitedly looking for their host families. Jacq, a tall blond, gregarious nineteen-year-old boy from Holland, quickly located us, and we began a hectic but fascinating week. We soon became fast friends as we shared family meals, swapped interesting stories, and got to know each other and our different cultures.

Jacq had brought many color pictures of his family, his high school, his hometown, and other landmarks all over the Netherlands. He told us all about the educational system, the climate and economy, and everyday life in his country. He was full of information!

Justin, Chris, and Alison were particularly interested in what a teenager's life was like in Holland.

Jacq had lots of questions for us and observations about America from his visits with families in other parts of the country on the "Up With People" tour. He even went to Alison's sixth-grade class as a guest and shared with the students his experiences growing up as a Dutch boy in his native land. After his week at our house, Jacq wrote a gracious note of thanks, but we felt that we were the ones who had benefited the most from his visit.

Getting to know Jacq was such a positive experience, we decided to invite an international student from the University of Southern Maine to spend Christmas weekend with us. Zhu Hong, a petite, dark-haired young woman from Shanghai, was a bright freshman economics major. Although she had been in America for over a semester, she had not yet been in an American home. Having grown up in Communist China, she was eager to celebrate her first Christmas.

After her arrival at our home, Alison and Chris asked Zhu Hong if she would like to go ice skating with them on the outdoor rink in town. She had never been on a pair of ice skates in her life, but was eager to try the sport. Bundled up warmly, she borrowed my skates, and off they all went. Later, we made our traditional Fuller holiday "sprinkle cookies" together, and Zhu Hong helped me chop vegetables as I prepared the Christmas Eve buffet. Alison taught our guest Christmas carols on the piano, and Zhu Hong participated in our family traditions of candlelighting, caroling, and reading of the Christmas story from the Bible.

On Christmas day, after opening presents, having a late-morning brunch, and going for a walk in the snow, Zhu Hong showed us a full-length video of life in Shanghai and Beijing which she had filmed and narrated before leaving her homeland. We saw interesting images of the inside of university dorms, bustling city streets crowded with bicycles — even a college dance. We learned things about the Far East we had never known before. Zhu Hong also gave us gifts from China as a bond of friendship, and we have kept in touch through cards ever since we moved away.

International Students in the U.S.

In any given year, several hundred thousand young people from more than 175 countries are in the United States to pursue undergraduate or graduate studies. They are among the most intelligent and promising youngsters in their native countries and will return as leaders. Zhu Hong, for example, was one of 80 top students in Shanghai, a city of millions. These gifted young people come to America not only to study in our colleges and universities, but also to learn about our people, customs, and way of life. And they can learn that best from visits with a family rather than remaining isolated in a dormitory with other international students.

As Rie Honjo, a Japanese student, said in a letter she wrote before she arrived for a scheduled visit at our house: "I am eager to be a member of your family for five days. And I want to learn various things about Oklahoma and learn better English speaking. So please help me."

But many of these international students never get to see the inside of an American home. Instead they spend lonely holidays in nearly deserted dormitories far from home without friends or family.

189

Building Bridges

We can all make a great difference in the experience of international students in America. We can build bridges of friendship that will last for years. Not only that, but hosting a guest from another country has tremendous benefits for us and our children. Whether our visitor has been from Taiwan, Japan, Holland, or China, we have found that the blessing of hosting foreign friends is a two-way street. We all learn together and our children's motivation for learning geography and the culture of other nations is boosted.

In this family adventure, you and your child will not only learn more about the international guest personally, but will also benefit from a greater knowledge of and appreciation for the customs, education, climate, attitudes, and way of life of her foreign homeland. Such exchanges will also help you and your family to begin to see our American lifestyle through the eyes of a visitor from another country and perspective — always an enlightening experience!

Kelly Hagan, nineteen, is a member of an Oklahoma family who has hosted many international visitors. She also has been an exchange student in Japan. "When our Japanese visitors were here and we took them to the Cowboy Hall of Fame," she notes, "we looked at things so differently; we noticed things we had taken for granted. We looked at the Fourth of July parade through their eyes, and afterward they showed us pictures of their Japanese festival days, parades, traditional dances, and kimono dress."

Kirk and Kendall Hagan, Kelly's parents, lived in England for six years. Upon their return to America they found that they missed the contact with other cultures. So they began hosting international students and adults. As they opened their home and hearts to foreign guests, the Hagan family developed many long-term friendships with people from France, Russia, Mexico, Holland, Japan, and England.

Having the many international guests in their home through their growing-up years also motivated Kelly and brother Kevin to study foreign languages. Kelly converses readily in French and Japanese, and Kevin in French and Spanish.

Reaching Out

By visiting in a home, the international student has an opportunity for friendship and involvement with an American family. Also, for the student just arriving from abroad, a host family is a great help in getting over the initial "culture shock." She has someone to help ease the difficult transition and to interpret some of the different (and perhaps bizarre!) things she encounters in her new and often bewildering environment. Most of all, a relationship with a host family serves as an antidote for the homesickness and loneliness the student often feels when she discovers herself alone thousands of miles from home in a strange land, culture, and language.

"Thanks for your kindness and everything you did," wrote Kiyori, an international student from Japan who came to visit us with Rie. "I lived with you for only five days, but I had happy life with you. Especially I liked Fourth of July Picnic, Parade and choir concert. In Oklahoma City the people were very friendly and kind."

What Kiyori and Rie wanted most was to learn to speak more conversational English. That was difficult because although they had studied English for seven years in school, they could speak and understand little of our language. Our idioms were particularly difficult for them to grasp. They had a better command of written English.

So I had the idea that music might be the key to helping them learn more spoken English. After a dinner at a Wendy's restaurant one night (they loved Wendy's hamburgers — almost as much as they loved shopping and paddle-boat riding at the pond), I got out my guitar, wrote down the words for them to follow, and taught them some traditional American folksongs like "You Are My Sunshine," "I've Been Working on the Railroad," and "Row, Row, Row Your Boat." Their favorite American song (first heard in Japan) was "Jesus Loves the Little Children of the World." They sang Japanese songs for us and we recorded our song session because they wanted to take the tape back to Japan and practice.

Kiyori and Rie showed us photographs of their families, schools, and friends, as well as pictures of cities (like Tokyo and Hiroshima), Shinto shrines and temples, and the fabulous mountains of Japan. We learned that the typical Japanese diet has much less fat than the average American diet, and that prices on cosmetics and other consumer items are much higher in Japan. We also found that Kiyori and Rie didn't like to walk as fast as we did in the shopping mall! Our gentle, gracious Oriental friends taught us some Japanese words and greatly enriched and enlivened our lives.

Kiyori and Rie introduced Alison to Origami, the Japanese paper-folding art, by leaving delicate orange and red paper cranes and rabbits on her pillow. In addition, they left behind several packages of the bright-colored Origami paper. Soon afterwards, we found a book with diagrams showing how to do Origami, which became a summer hobby for Alison.

Getting in Touch

Here are some suggestions in case you are interested in inviting an international student to your home:

To get in touch with a student, call the international student office or foreign student advisor on the college or university campus nearest you, or contact Youth for Understanding, American Field Service or your local Chamber of Commerce.

There are short-term visits in your home for a designated period — a holiday, weekend or week — like the five-day exchange in July between Bunka Women's University, Tokyo, and Oklahoma City University in which we participated. And there are long-term arrangements in which the student does not actually live in your home but is assigned to you for a period of a year during which time you act as host family in the community providing on-going care and friendship for the student. You meet your foreign guest upon her arrival in this country, invite her for occasional family dinners, and include her in community events. Some host families have their student over once a month, while others get together more frequently.

Smoothing Cross-Cultural Exchanges

A smoother cross-cultural exchange will be established and maintained if you will follow these simple suggestions:*

- Talk slowly and clearly with your new foreign friend. If she doesn't understand, repeat what you are trying to say in simpler, more formal English, using fewer slang words and fewer idiomatic expressions (such as "run to the store," "grab a bite of lunch," "or "hop

---

*Some of these suggestions are adapted from: "Host Family Ministry," National Student Ministries, 127 Ninth Avenue North, Nashville, TN 37234.

a plane"). Avoid the common practice of raising your voice to make yourself understood; foreign students are not deaf or simple-minded and will not appreciate being treated as though they were. Although effective oral communication may be difficult at first, don't be afraid to try it. Be patient and kind; try to put yourself in your international guest's shoes and imagine how you would feel in a totally foreign country, culture, and language.

- Telephone in advance when you invite her to share a meal or some family activity in order to give her plenty of time to fit the event into her schedule of classes, study, and work and to arrange personal transportation.

- Show an interest in your student by encouraging her to talk about herself — her family, customs, education, home life, religion, ambitions, hopes, and plans. She may have pictures or maps she would like to show if you ask. When she shares about her life and country, be a good listener.

- Ask her to teach you a greeting, song or other words in her language. You may consider teaching her an American song.

- Ask what she would like to see or do in your community.

- If possible, let her bring a friend some time for dinner or get together with another host family and their international guest.

- Include the student in Thanksgiving, Christmas, and other holiday celebrations.

- After you've gotten to know each other better, ask your foreign friend if she would like to come to your home and prepare a traditional meal from her country.

- Don't feel that you always have to entertain the visitor. She may enjoy just taking part in regular family activities, including doing chores, helping prepare meals, and spending a quiet time reading, studying, or writing letters.

- If problems arise, consult the foreign student advisor on campus.

- If possible, read about your guest's home country. The knowledge you gain will increase the value and enjoyment of your shared experience. An encyclopedia and other books from the library can provide lots of background facts and data. Other helpful sources of information on foreign countries are:

Other Lands, Other Peoples

National Education Association of the U.S.
1201 16th Street, N.W.
Washington, D.C. 20006 ($2.25 per copy)

"Background Notes"
The Superintendent of Documents
U.S. Government Printing Office
Washington, D.C. 20402 (5 cents a pamphlet on each
country; $6.00 for the
whole series)

A Little Child Will Lead Them

Children make great hosts and hostesses for international students. With their natural curiosity, enthusiasm and lack of inhibitions, often they can help overcome cultural barriers and build bridges of understanding. Their spontaneity and lack of self-consciousness makes a visitor feel at ease.

Alison, our youngest, was the most outgoing of the family in the presence of our international guests. Having only brothers, she was delighted to have two new Japanese "sisters" sharing her room for a week. Although at first she and they could communicate very little in words, Alison accompanied our Japanese guests on an afternoon visit to a local shopping mall and discovered a favorite universal pastime shared by girls of all ages and nationalities — shopping. She also took her new "sisters" bike riding, swimming, and to an amusement park.

Alison still has a shoe box filled with mementos of visits by Kiyori and Rie and other international guests. She has saved their letters, especially the foreign stamps which she eagerly hoards for her collection.

Motivating Children to Learn Geography

Learning geography doesn't have to be merely a school-time activity. In fact, children of all ages are much more motivated to learn the location of countries, states, oceans, and rivers if they see a reason to do so — because their family has an interest in people and cultures in other parts of the world, because they know someone from another country, or because they have read about other nations and nationalities. Then geography is no longer just a bunch of meaningless, unconnected facts which they have to learn by rote.

American students traditionally score very low in geography, but here are some ways to take the drudgery out of your child's learning this important subject:

- Place a large world map on the wall in the family work room (or even in the child's bedroom). Maps are a valuable resource in geographic study. If there is some event on the news, like the Berlin Wall coming down or a riot in Beijing, you can easily call the incident to the child's attention and say, "Let's see where that took place; can you find it?" If there is severe weather in some part of the country or globe, or if an important environmental issue such as the Alaskan oil spill is on the evening news, you and your child can look together to see where it is taking place.

If your child is studying a particular country in social studies, you can ask her to point it out to you on the map. Laminated maps are great because you can write on them or plot the route of a trip with a washable marker and then later erase it.

You can also spark an interest in geography by using thumbtacks to attach to the map the name or picture of relatives or friends who are visiting, moving to or living in different parts of the United States or world.

In the Hemry family, Ken plots his route on the map when he goes on a business trip so daughters Lauren and Heather will gain a sense of where he is and develop an interest in geography. Before the family goes on a trip, they plot their route together on the map. (String or an erasable highlighter can be used for this purpose.)

As the Hemrys travel or go for a ride, Ken shows the girls how to orient themselves on the ground so that they can find where the car is parked in a large lot. He points out prominent objects near the vehicle to get them used to looking for familiar landmarks. As the family drives around in the city, they talk about street and traffic signs and what they mean.

- Buy some soft stuffed globes in bright colors which your younger child can play with or use as pillows.

- Equip the child's room with wooden and cardboard puzzles of the United States and countries of the world. These are great for children of all ages. Manipulating a piece and talking about the place it represents and the products which come from that area (which may be indicated on the individual pieces) makes learning geography both painless and enjoyable.

- Pick up some of the numerous games which help children become more aware of geography. These can be used to help your child learn a great deal about the physical world while having fun in the process. Some popular geography games are:

"Where in the World?"

"IQ World Geography"

"IQ United States Geography"

"Worldwide Pen Pals"

"World Traveller"

"Geo Safari" (electronic game)

These games, as well as geography flash cards, are available at learning resource stores and many retail toy outlets. With the geography cards (which match city and state, or country and city), children can play concentration or make up their own games.

- When you travel, play a license plate game. Give each child in the car a copy of a U.S. map and crayons. When a youngster spots a license plate from a particular state, she gets to color in that state on her map. The one who has the most states colored at the end of the trip is the winner.

- On long trips, you can also let your child play navigator. Allow her to hold the road map and help you figure out which route to take to reach your destination, where you should stop for gas or lunch, and how long it will take to get to a certain place or landmark (like Grandma's house).

If you will follow these suggestions and make an effort to show a personal interest in other nations and nationalities, keep abreast of world events and international affairs, and continue to learn about your own country, region, state and city, your child will grow up with a wider knowledge of geography and a greater awareness and appreciation of different world cultures.

Chapter 15

OVERCOMING MOTIVATION BUSTER #1: A LACK OF ATTENTION SKILLS

"On your mark, get set, go!" we would call out before a childhood race.

A child who is ready for learning begins by focusing his attention. But a major roadblock to learning for many children is a lack of attention skills. The child who has great difficulty focusing and concentrating on a task is at a disadvantage in the classroom and often loses motivation for learning.

Luke Garvey was enthusiastic and ready to learn when he began school. He was one of the youngest students in the class, yet bright and capable. By the time he reached second grade, however, his mother was getting weekly notes from his teacher: "Luke is not getting his work done; he is just not motivated." "Luke is restless and inattentive."

Luke also developed behavior problems. After several parent-teacher conferences, he was tested at school, but his IQ was above average. No signs of learning disabilities were found. The problems continued. By the spring, Luke was behind in reading and his teacher recommended that he be retained in second grade.

Luke began second grade again in a large class of thirty-two children. Surely, his mother thought, now he will settle down and enjoy school. But soon the notes were being sent home again: "Luke is not finishing his seatwork." "Luke can't sit still; he has a hard time staying on a task."

By this time, Luke hated school and his self-esteem had plummeted. After having him evaluated by a pediatrician and an educational psychologist, his parents were told that he suffered from Attention Deficit Disorder.

Like Luke, many children in the United States (an estimated ten percent of the school population) show signs of this "fidgety syndrome." By early 1990, experts say, over one million children in America will be on medication to control attention deficit and hyperactivity problems.

Six to nine times as many boys as girls have difficulty concentrating. Children from ages six to nine are most likely to be described as having attentional problems, which show up as the demands of the school day increase.

What Are the Characteristics of ADD?

The American Psychiatric Association says that ADD (Attention Deficit Disorder) is indicated when a child shows problems with inattention, impulsivity, and/or hyperactivity. Children with ADD may have an average or above-average IQ, and some have learning disabilities. Although each child is very individual, the two main classifications of children with attentional problems are: ADD without hyperactivity (about twenty percent of cases, more frequently girls) and ADD with hyperactivity (about eighty percent of cases, more often boys). The ADD symptoms may be mild, moderate, or severe.

ADD without hyperactivity: Meg's teachers always described her as "quietly inattentive" and "daydreamy." She was not disruptive in the classroom, but didn't seem to listen or be "tuned in." Meg missed directions, had trouble getting started, and rarely stuck to a task. Easily distracted, she forgot books or homework assignments, so her school work suffered. On the playground, she had difficulty with team activities.

ADD with hyperactivity: Jake was an over-active child. His mother called him her "little dynamo" who, from the age of eleven months, ran about and climbed on everything. In the classroom, he had difficulty sitting still, was distractible and always "on the go." He seemed to continually drum his fingers or tap his foot. His teacher said that he was "driven like a motor." Clumsy, aggressive, and unable to wait his turn, he was left out of the games and sports engaged in by children his age. He was often impulsive and had difficulty organizing his work. When anxious or stressed, Jake became out of control.

What Are the Causes of Attention Problems?

Although researchers stress that there is no conclusive evidence of the causes of attention problems, Randi Hagerman, M.D., of the Child Development Unit of the Children's Hospital, Denver, Colorado, says that many children show a genetic predisposition to attentional problems and hyperactivity. These youngsters usually have parents or siblings with similar problems.

But there is strong evidence that children who have recurrent middle-ear infections in infancy and as toddlers are much more likely to have auditory processing and attentional problems, says Dr. Hagerman. "There is a trend in our society for more mothers to work and put their kids in day care. In day care children get exposed to a lot of infectious diseases, have more middle-ear infections, and this places them at a high risk for attentional problems."

More rigid academic demands on early elementary school children may also be part of the problem. Doctors report that they are seeing more children in the first through third grades who are referred for attentional problems and hyperactivity as a result of being stressed and expected to do things they're not ready to handle. Even four- to six-year-olds spend a great deal of time at desks doing drills and worksheets and facing rigorous tests, which experts like Dr. David Elkind of Tufts University say will only create more long-term learning problems.

What ADD Is Not

Sometimes the label "Attention Deficit" is attached to a child who is overplaced or given work beyond his ability. Children who are developmentally young for their grade level can easily be misdiagnosed by impatient adults, points out one physician. These youngsters don't need to be on medication; they need time, instruction, patience, and support by teachers and parents. Like the little lion in "Leo the Late Bloomer," these children will learn, bloom, and shine as their inner timeclocks and developmental needs are respected.

Mourning after a major loss such as death or divorce can cause a child to show less concentration, a shortened attention span, and distractability. And these behaviors inevitably lead to school problems. During such a period of mourning (which may last a year), a young person needs a support system: understanding parents, an extended family, close friends, patient teachers, and perhaps even counseling and reassurance that the attention problems are temporary.

Family turmoil, chronic depression, and anxiety all make it difficult for young people to focus and concentrate. Dr. Darrel Lang of Emporia State University in Kansas, who has studied stress in thousands of school-age children, finds a high correlation between the negative effects of stress and tension and the evidence of attention problems and hyperactivity. Tension causes an inability to focus. When this problem arises, it calls for a look at the child's family life and problems.

When a child is having problems in school, parents have to be careful not to attribute everything to neurological problems or disorders, says Dr. David Elkind. "The first thing to do is always to look at the child's whole life and what is going on. Is the child totally scheduled and under constant time pressure? Is he having trouble with peers or having trouble with a teacher? Is the family under stress or having problems? Look at all of those things first instead of immediately jumping on a child for being hyperactive and needing medication. I find that too often. When the child is upset or overactive, check out everything else before you consider medication."

There are other physical conditions which have similar symptoms. "A child who is hyperthyroid may look very hyperactive with all kinds of attentional and learning problems," says Dr. Hagerman. Food allergies can cause overactivity and mimic attention problems.

When Christopher was five, he was in a serious car accident. Soon afterwards, he began to have problems in kindergarten — impulsiveness, hyperactive behavior, mood swings. A neurologist recommended that he be sent to an ADD clinic. After extensive evaluation, the doctors found that Christopher's problems were due mainly to severe allergies to over 25 different foods, molds, and inhalants. After eliminating all sugar and caffeine, and being placed on a rotation diet, Christopher was able to function happily in the classroom and at home.*

So it is very important to have a thorough physical examination, neurodevelopmental assessment, and medical history before making any diagnosis of attention deficit. As parents, we should always be careful to look into the *reasons* for the attention problems of our children.

How Do We Help Children With ADD?

"Medication should never be the first alternative," says Norma Sturniolo, M.A., special education coordinator for the Yarmouth, Maine, schools. "Education needs to be the first alternative, followed by modifications in the programs both at school and home to meet the needs of the child. Then if these things are not working, we consider the situation a medical problem."

Some children have been helped with medication. The most popular is Ritalin, a central-nervous stimulant which produces a paradoxical calming effect in hyperactive or ADD children. Dexedrine and Cylert are also commonly

---

*For a guide to help children who suffer from allergies and food or chemical sensitivities which interfere with learning and normal behavior, see the book *The Impossible Child* by Doris J. Rapp, published by Practical Allergy Research Foundation, P.O. Box 60, Buffalo, New York 14223-0060.

prescribed. Although not a cure for all of a child's school problems, in some cases stimulants do seem to improve focusing ability and motor coordination.

"But remember, medication is not a magic pill. It does not make people learn, and it does not make them smarter," says Andy Watry, executive director of the George State Board of Medical Examiners. "All it does technically is to help them in the evaluative thinking process to weed out some of the stray signals so they can focus on a task and not be diverted by every little thing that goes on around them."

We need to ask: What can be done to help a child with attention problems without resorting to medication? What can the school do to address the problem? What can parents do at home (including changing the child's diet)?

Homeschooling is an alternative some families are choosing.

From the earliest grades, Jeremy had problems in school. His teachers described him as disruptive and inattentive. "He doesn't seem to intentionally be out of control; I think it's something chemical," said more than one of his teachers. So when he was in the second grade, after consulting with a doctor, Jeremy's parents put him on medication.

As he grew in size, the dosage had to be increased and Jeremy began to display severe side effects — he developed facial tics, suffered from chronic sleeplessness, and acted like a zombie at school. His classroom problems were not abated by the medication. In the third and forth grades, his teachers said of him: "He disrupts the flow of things," and "He can't keep up." Jeremy's parents tried placing him in both public and private Christian schools, but the work was overwhelming and he made failing grades in spite of the fact that his achievement test and IQ scores were very high (on the post-high school level in reading, vocabulary, etc.).

Social interaction at school was a disaster for Jeremy. He was picked on and ostracized by the other students. His self-esteem plummeted to a low point, and the side effects of the medication made matters even more difficult for him.

So when he reached the sixth grade, Jeremy's parents took him off the medication and began homeschooling him. At first his mother worked on filling in the gaps in his knowledge of math (like how to handle problems in long division) before they could move on to higher math. She integrated literature and history into his schedule. Jeremy was an avid reader and loved all science. With the one-to-one instruction provided by homeschooling, he made progress in all subjects.

Jeremy had time to develop friendships through youth group activities at church, a big homeschool group which met for sports and other events every Friday, his local Boy Scout troop, and in piano lessons. He also helped with children his mother cared for in the afternoons when his own reading and learning projects were completed. Now almost fourteen, Jeremy shows a higher self-esteem, enjoys greater success in his studies, and has found renewed interest in his school work.

When all else fails, Andy Watry says, there are those children who may need medication to function in a classroom setting. But even then, the parent should consider using a conservative treatment approach, making sure that there is appropriate monitoring.

In addition, modifications (like small group work, individual tutoring, special education classes at school, and individual and family therapy) can work together to benefit the child. Whether or not medication is indicated, the child with attention problems needs help building his listening skills and attention span, and, most of all, boosting his self-esteem.

Questions a Parent Needs to Ask Before a Child Is Put On Stimulant Medication*

1. What condition does the child have?

A thorough physical, educational, and neurological assessment with a medical and developmental history can reveal the condition of the child and the reason for his attentional problems or hyperactivity. Prescriptions made on the basis of a brief interview and ten-minute exam should be avoided. Also, the child's diet should be considered. (Before he is placed on medication, sugar — and especially caffeine — should be eliminated.)

2. Are there other alternatives to medication? Are there any special learning programs, counseling techniques, or home activities that would help?

The decision to recommend medication should not be made until there is reasonable assurance that the child's problem does not stem from overplacement, boredom, poor teaching, or an inadequate school environment.

3. If medication is prescribed, what other intervention (counseling, modifications at school and at

---

home, special education, tutoring, etc.) is planned to help the child?

4. What are the risks of this drug, and what are the benefits?

Parents need to discuss with their physician the risks and benefits of medication, along with any possible side effects of the drug (which can include suppressed appetite, increased heart and blood pressure, headaches and/or stomach aches, and delayed growth).

5. If medication is prescribed, how will it be monitored?

Physicians agree that the lowest dosage possible is best. A low dosage can help develop the child's attention span and motor coordination. A higher dosage, which may regulate behavior, actually retards learning and puts the child at greater risk from side effects. A child who is overdosed may become violent or aggressive with peers, go on "crying jags," display moodiness or irritability, or become chronically depressed.

Close communication between physician, parent, and teacher is important. While the child is on medication, a regular six-month check-up is essential, with heart and blood pressure checked and weight and height growth monitored.

---

*Questions suggested by Andy Watry, executive director of the Georgia State Board of Medical Examiners.

Here are several suggestions of what to do at home to help the child with attention problems:

1. Provide a stable, secure, controlled environment with structured opportunities for fun and study.

- The child's room needs to be organized: lots of shelves and labels on drawers, his own bulletin board with reminders for routines and special activities, an uncluttered desk to do school work. He needs a storage box near the door for "school stuff": backpack, boots, mittens, gymclothes, a snack for the next day. Then the child feels an inner sense of order and is better able to focus.

- It is important to establish a household routine and consistent guidelines and limits for the child's behavior. Lack of consistent, loving discipline and limit-setting in the early years causes the child to fail to learn self-control, thus aggravating his attention problems.*

- It is likewise essential to limit environmental noises in the home. Lower the volume on home entertainment equipment and don't mix television, stereo, radio, and video game output. Television reinforces non-listening and short attention span. Instead of letting him watch too much TV, encourage the child to participate in games like Parcheesi, Memory, Pictionary. Provide him plenty of puzzles and

---

*The need for loving discipline by parents is an important factor in encouraging motivated, capable children. Both overly rigid discipline and overly permissive parenting tends to be a roadblock to motivation and learning. Excellent reading on the subject is James Dobson's *Dare To Discipline* and H. Stephen Glenn's *Raising Self-Reliant Children in a Self-Indulgent World*.

instructional toys like Lego blocks. Playing games helps him learn to follow directions and to sustain attention while trying to reach a concrete goal.

- A few times each week have a quiet reading time with the child, making sure that distractions are reduced to a minimum. (Be sensitive to the amount of time he can concentrate at one stretch; begin with a short period and then gradually lengthen his reading assignment by adding a page or two each day.)

Ms. Sturniolo suggests focusing on the child, directing his attention to the story line in a high-interest book: "I'm going to read a couple of pages. The little girl in the story is going to have something happen to her. I want you to listen for what it is." Then after reading a few pages and hearing his response, ask, "What do you predict is going to happen next?" Reading aloud helps the child develop listening and attention skills, and the time spent together boosts the youngster's sense of self-esteem.

- Prepare your child for what is going to happen. "The Smiths are coming for dinner tonight." "In ten minutes we are leaving for the library; soon you can start putting away your Legos." Verbal cueing reduces anxiety, says Kerry Jones, a reading specialist.

- Keep instructions short. Give them one at a time, gradually adding another as the child's attention span grows.

- If the child is physically overactive, provide him outlets to work off extra energy: a play-break after school, a chance to jump on the rebounder, a bike ride, or a jog before study time.

- Play "Twenty Questions," "I Spy," and "Simon Says" to improve the youngster's listening and attention skills. Have him listen to stories, poems, and songs on tape.

2. Boost the child's self-esteem. "Self-esteem is the key issue for every child. If he doesn't have good self-esteem, he will have a very hard time learning," says Ms. Sturniolo. Building self-esteem is especially important for children with attention problems because they receive more negative feedback at school and at home which batters their self-image.

- Build on your child's strengths. Emphasize and reinforce his talents, skills, and positive character traits. What does he enjoy doing? What is he good at? What are his special interests? Use the momentum of his enthusiasm to build a string of successes. Find out what he does best and encourage him in it!

Individual sports activities like swimming or tennis are often better than competitive team sports.

If your child has an interest in music, get him involved in lessons. Musical activities help children develop physical coordination, timing, memory, and visual and auditory skills. Even playing a simple recorder or drumming to music helps a youngster focus his attention and builds mental concentration.

Art is particularly important for ADD children. Drawing may be frustrating, but hands-on activities like sculpting in clay, knitting or weaving, working with textures or collages captures their attention and helps them build attention skills.

- Collections are valuable resources. Encourage the child to collect whatever interests him: rocks, baseball cards, shells. Collecting enhances organizing skills and helps the child become an "expert" at something.

- A daily chore or chores that the child is responsible for carrying out encourages initiative and the finishing of assigned tasks. (Often when a child gets sidetracked and doesn't complete jobs, the parent takes on the responsibilities, thus *decreasing* the youngster's sense of self-esteem.)

- Provide lots of positive reinforcement and patient love. Encourage eye contact and both visual and verbal expression. Home needs to be a place where the child knows he is unconditionally loved, accepted, and listened to, a place where he can make a mistake and be forgiven.

Concentrating is difficult for some ADD children because their learning style is *active* rather than passive. For the active or kinesthetic learner, try making up a cheer for spelling words, bouncing a basketball while repeating the multiplication tables, playing charades with vocabulary words. Practice writing math facts on a large chalkboard. Let the child learn and study by seeing, hearing, and doing. In addition, try these study tips for the child who has trouble concentrating:

- Eliminate all distractions during a daily study time.

- Have the child read the material to you, another adult, or an older sibling.

- Suggest that the child set small, acceptable goals, like "After I learn these five states and capitals, I'm going outside to play a while." For a longer assignment, have the child make a calendar to break down the task into steps and place a sticker on each step completed.

- Many children with attention problems have trouble organizing. "I have a big report in science due tomorrow and I don't know how to start." I lost my math papers." Help your child learn organization by providing him color-coded folders for each subject (or use any notebook and assignment system that works for him).

3. Work with the school.

- Cooperate with your child's teacher and school personnel on individualized education plans. Visit the classroom, observe the child's educational setting, and consider whether it is providing what he needs. "You'll need to be an advocate for your child throughout his school years," says Mr. Sturniolo. Keep up communication with the teacher and share what you are doing and what seems to be working at home.

- Focus on effort, not grades. Encourage your child with statements like: "I'm proud of how hard you've worked on your science project." "This work shows great improvement!" "You're really learning!"

- Build on strengths rather than magnifying weaknesses. Don't label the child with technical names for disorders. Instead, be specific about what the problem is: "I know it's hard for you to pay attention, but this is what we must do now," or, "I know it's hard for you to stay calm and concentrate, but here's something that will help."

- Most of all, enjoy your child and his unique personality, gifts, and achievements — big and little.

With home and school working together, your child can grow and learn to meet the challenges that lie ahead, take problems in stride, and become productive and happy.

Chapter 16

OVERCOMING MOTIVATION BUSTER #2: ABSENCE DUE TO SICKNESS

- Matt, a sixth-grader, broke his leg, was placed in traction, and was ordered to stay off his feet; he missed almost six weeks of school.

- Holly underwent kidney surgery and had to be out of school for five weeks.

- John has missed several weeks of school intermittently throughout the semester due to chronic asthma problems.

It does take some effort and planning, but if your child becomes ill and has to miss school, especially for a week or more, learning does not have to be interrupted.

One of my eighth-grade students, Kathy, got the flu and missed two weeks of school. The third week the illness went into bronchitis. The fourth week Kathy dreaded coming back to school and was depressed. Neither of her parents called to ask for her assignments and homework. Although we sent home the class novel for her to read, along with make-up work, and called to keep in touch and to see if she needed any help, Kathy didn't turn in the required papers and projects within the period of time allotted. There was no parent at home during the day to supervise and encourage her to finish assignments, so she spent the majority of her time off watching soap operas and game shows on television.

When Kathy came back to school, she was behind in every subject. She had been a B and C student, but soon became discouraged and overwhelmed when she failed make-ups tests and faced the volume of work she had to catch up on. Although I tried to work with Kathy after school, her motivation fell to a low-ebb and she just began to give up. She ended up losing an entire semester of work and having to go to summer school.

In contrast, Michael was forced to miss two whole months of school due to confinement in a body cast as a result of injuries he had received in a serious car accident. He had been an average student at best, but during the time he was at home recuperating, he was given special help by a tutor whom his parents and the school had arranged to visit three times a week. Besides doing his required reading and assigned written work, Michael practiced his guitar in bed. When he returned to school and completed his tests and deferred projects, Michael's grades had actually improved and he was more motivated than he had ever been about academics and preparation for college.

What made the difference? Parental support, encouragement, and involvement. If parents and teachers cooperate, a student who must miss class for an extended time can still keep up with her school work, complete her studies, and stay motivated for learning. Individual, one-on-one help from the parent or teacher can benefit the child, and she can even make great progress during her absence from school.

Whether a short-term, temporary illness (such as the flu, mumps, strep-throat, or chicken pox) or a long-term chronic sickness (like rheumatoid arthritis, diabetes, asthma, or, as in the case of my friend Marilyn's daughter, cystic fibrosis), juvenile medical disorders do not have to result in lower grades, lack of achievement, retention in the same grade or class the next school year, or loss of credit for courses in high school.

Making the Most of "Sick Time"

Through several years of dealing with absences caused by our son's chronic, severe asthma, and after talking with other parents in the same situation, I learned some secrets of how to make the time spent at home go faster, help keep children motivated and current with school work, and ease the transition when they return to school (in short, to "make lemonade when handed a lemon"):

1. If your child misses any more than two days of school, ask that each of her teachers write out her assignments. Make provision for a student to gather the textbooks and materials the child will need, and arrange for a time to have them picked up.

If the illness becomes more extended, a homebound teacher may be able to provide instruction. Sometimes the child's regular teacher will volunteer to come to the home after school or in the evening once or twice a week to instruct and encourage her and to help her keep up with her studies — if the teacher is made aware of the situation.

A retired teacher in your church might volunteer to tutor your child is some subjects, or an older high school or college student may be willing to help out for a nominal fee.

When our son Justin was sick, my husband and I split up the responsibilities of tutoring and explaining certain subjects. In the evening, Holmes helped Justin with science and math, and in the afternoon I tutored him in English and history.

2. Go to the library and check out a stack of high-interest books and magazines that will appeal to your child or teenager and spark her interest. (For variety, change these out every two weeks or so.) Without the distractions of a hectic school schedule, your child can develop a love for reading she may never have otherwise discovered.

During a time of illness, books like photographic histories of America or science volumes with colorful pictures can be especially enjoyable. The parents' old high school or college yearbooks and photo albums are often fun to peruse during long, boring afternoons.

If your child likes athletics, stock up on sports biographies and magazines. If she is interested in animals, find books to stimulate that interest. Collections of stories, myths, poems — put these in a basket beside the child's bed or on a bedside table. Make sure there is good lighting, and a bedside lamp for evening and nighttime reading.

If feverish, the child shouldn't do much reading or engage in a lot of visual activities. During this time, someone in the family can read aloud to the patient at least once a day. At other times, story or book tapes from the library can be played.

After the fever subsides, encourage the child to read from the great stock of books and magazines you've supplied, and continue to read aloud to her. If a novel or book report has been assigned as part of her make-up work, you can read aloud together a chapter each day and talk about the plot, characters, setting, and theme of the book as the story unfolds.

3. Provide some structure for the child who is ill or recovering. Set up a schedule for the week days which includes time for school work, reading for pleasure, play (see ideas below), craft work, or the making of something the child enjoys (perhaps the writing of a thank-you note or a letter to a friend), and leisure activities such as watching television.

"Sometimes Rebekah is homebound for two weeks at a time due to intravenous medication and four hours of daily treatments for infections from cystic fibrosis," says her mother, Marilyn Phillips. "To keep her motivated, I've found it to be essential to allow her to have relaxing time to do what she wants, as well as structured learning times. I have found it best to schedule a daily time just to do school work, and to allot a period for recreational reading. Rebekah does well when she knows that at certain times of the day no TV is allowed because 'this is school work time.' By having a scheduled time for every activity, Rebekah is fresh and willing to do her work. I try to make it a positive experience and reward her with stickers or stamps when she has done well."

Too much television derails the engine of motivation, so try to limit TV watching. Lying in bed all day consuming the usual television fare results in boredom, apathy and falling behind in school work. Allowing the child to choose a certain (parent approved) television show to watch, followed by an alloted time for work after the set is turned off, is helpful. Educational television programs on science (like a series on panda bears or dolphins), history, or geography are motivating. You can encourage your child to write a little summary of the program to share with her teacher or the family in the evening.

A long day alone can go by very slowly for a child or teen, so if you must be outside the home for a while, have someone in the immediate or extended family or a neighbor or friend from church be there part of the day to visit with the child, play a board game with her, or read to her. Leave an assignment sheet and calendar with ideas for what the child can do that day. Have set times during the day that you call the child on the telephone and visit. Perhaps her teacher can come by aiter school and share a get-well card the whole class has made (this can bring a big smile to a child who feels lonely and isolated).

Meeting emotional needs by taking time to listen to your child's feelings and thoughts and by doing something enjoyable together is also an important part of the recovery process. When children are sick, they need special times when they know their parents are "there" for them.

"It helps a child stay motivated when sick at home for his parents to show a real interest in what he is doing, asking in a positive and interested way to see what he has been working on, and checking it over," says Gayle, a homebound teacher. Saying something encouraging about a paper or worksheet also helps.

4. Remember that busy hands are happy hands. Provide a tote bag beside the bed with creative activities for your child: paper dolls and play dough for the younger child, a sketch pad for the older youngster. A small chalkboard with felt glued to one side can make a good

surface on which to arrange and play with cut-out letters, animals, and shapes. A tray or lapboard provides a flat surface for working puzzles, cutting up magazines, and free-hand drawing.

To keep these things organized and avoid a messy bed, you can put them in Zip-lock bags, which also helps keep loose materials where they can be easily found: one bag for gluestick and scissors for making a scrapbook of pictures and another bag for crayons; a bag for sewing cards, or for cross-stitch embroidery for the older youngster. A shoe box can be used to hold Legos or little alphabet blocks and wooden animals.

For the older child or teen, provide some paper and envelopes for use in writing notes to friends (the younger child can also write letters to friends in invented spelling or by dictating them to you). Add a crossword puzzle book, a math puzzle, playing cards for a game of Solitaire, a chess or checker board, or a Pente set to use in play with family members or visitors.

5. Keep up the child's spirits. Besides plenty of liquids, chicken soup, and medicine to help the body get well, a convalescing child also needs lots of encouragement, love, humor, and reassurance to keep her cheered up. Missing soccer games, parties, and other activities is frustrating. To keep the child from feeling lonesome and forgotten, you can write humorous get-well verses and cards, provide little surprises on her dinner tray, place a special flower on the bedside table, and call her if you have to be away for a while. A time of recovering from illness can be a close, loving time in which to fill up a child's emotional tank. It can also be profitable in teaching her how to care for someone else who is sick as she observes how she is lovingly cared for.

We can make learning, school work done at home, and catch-up time both motivating and interesting. "I have tried hard to make learning enjoyable for Rebekah during her times of illness," says Marilyn Phillips. "For instance, when we are working with spelling or vocabulary words, often I make up games with vocabulary and spelling words such as 'Tic-Tac-Toe' or 'Bingo' from the homework assignments."

Rebekah's friends have been delighted to come over to her house after school and play these homemade vocabulary and spelling games with her and to visit and share with her the events of the day.

Often a student who is sick at home gets lonely for classmates. Many schools have their own VCRs and recording equipment that could be used to tape classroom instructions and presentations. The sick child could enjoy learning along with the class. (Marilyn Phillips suggests that the parent, a teacher's aide, or an office worker operate the camera and send the tape home to the sick child.) An audio tape could be made of lectures and information the older student needs and sent home as a resource for study.

6. Stay in touch with the school. In this type of situation, communication is important. Do not lower your expectations for the child, and don't allow the teacher to lower her expectations either. Instead, assure her that your child can and will keep up with her work and do well, if everyone works together.

"When Rebekah is sick or hospitalized," says Marilyn, "I always schedule a conference with her teacher. I make sure that the teacher understands the nature of the illness and knows how long the recuperation period should take. I let her know that I am interested in helping my child keep up with the rest of the class. I request that she give Rebekah *only* the assignments that are necessary to keep on top of the subjects. (For example, writing spelling words five times daily may not be a necessary assignment.) I have found the teachers to be wonderful and cooperative."

The recovering child can be helped to avoid putting unrealistic expectations on herself. For example, once Rebekah returned to school after a long illness and, on her first day back, scored an eighty-five on a test. She was upset because she didn't make a hundred. When her mother helped her realize that eighty-five was a good grade, especially considering the fact that she had missed the entire week of classroom instruction and drill on that subject, Rebekah was contented and soon had raised her grades to the desired level.

When sickness interrupts school, it doesn't have to interrupt learning; in fact, with support from parents and teachers, the child can return to school after a bout with the flu, chicken pox, or mononucleosis (even after suffering the pain and inconvenience of a broken leg) caught up with her school work, and perhaps even ahead in her motivation and enthusiasm for learning.

Chapter 17

OVERCOMING MOTIVATION BUSTER #3: SCHOOL TRANSFERS

In one third-grade class I worked with recently there sat Michael, who had just moved to Oklahoma from Alabama. Kristen, I discovered, was moving in one week to Florida. In two weeks, Brett and his family would depart for Utah and his dad's new job. And Melanie was moving to a new house and school in the city!

American families are on the move, and it's very likely your child will have to change schools some time before graduation. Around twenty percent of school-age children and their families move each year. The average child changes schools several times in thirteen years of schooling (kindergarten through twelfth grade). Some children must move several times a year.

Helping a child get adjusted to a new school following a family relocation is important. With changes involving the loss of friends and familiar surroundings, adjustment to a new school, and the learning of different rules and curriculums, youngsters need all the help they can get in the "moving experience."

The Benefits of Moving

There seems to be a universal expectation that any move will be traumatic and disruptive. Such expectations can have a powerful effect on a child and may themselves negatively influence his achievement and classroom behavior.

Moving can have its benefits, too. In fact, for some children, moving can result in improved academic performance. They may be stimulated by change. The new teacher and support staff may better be able to meet the child's needs. Along with the necessary support, children should be given the message that they can and will adapt positively to a planned move.

For Amy, who lived in ten different cities and attended eight different schools by the time she had reached her sophomore year, one of the great things about moving to different parts of the country was the chance to get involved in activities unique to each area.

"In Minnesota I learned to ski and canoe. I also tried ice fishing and wilderness camping. In Arizona, where I live now, I'm doing a lot more swimming and horseback riding . . . . Moving has brought our family much closer together. In a new place, we are all in the same boat and have to be each other's best friend for a while," she says.

Our move from Oklahoma to Maine gave our children first-hand experience with New England geography, as we traveled through the mountains of New Hampshire and along the rocky coasts of Maine, maps in hand. Our son

Justin's love of history was boosted tremendously by field trips to Salem, Massachusetts, and to Hawthorne's House of Seven Gables. In Yarmouth, he also enjoyed tracing a ship captain's family history with original documents. Our children had the opportunity to try different sports — ice skating, hockey, and lacrosse. When Alison's class studied the ocean, they went on a low-tide marsh walk to observe sea creatures.

Learning to rise to meet the challenges presented by moving can prepare children for later changes in life. Moving can also serve to broaden their horizons and help them develop confidence. With the support of their parents and teachers, the way for a move can be smoothed and the adjustment of our children to a new school and environment made easier so they will continue to be motivated and to enjoy learning and developing.

Before the Move

Helping a child adjust to a new school starts *before* the move. In whatever ways you can, depending upon the age of the child, involve him in the preparation and process of moving. Have a family meeting to discuss the reason for the move, involve the child in the family's house-hunting plans, and answer any questions he might have. Although you and your spouse may be sad about leaving family and friends, recognize that your attitude is important in helping your child make a good adjustment. You can talk about the move in a supportive and direct way, helping the youngster see the positive aspects of the change.

In selecting a new home you should take into account the quality of the schools in the area. You can get information about local schools from real estate people, coworkers, friends, and other parents you meet in the new area. Real estate agents can also tell you about how the local public schools compare with private or Christian institutions in the vicinity. You can sit in on a few classes your child would be in and talk to his prospective teachers. You can ask about facilities or programs for your child's favorite sport or particular skill. Especially for younger children, you should ask about the methods used in teaching reading and math. Either visit or write ahead and compare schools from different districts, keeping these questions in mind:

- What are the facilities like?

- What is the extent of special programs, such as those for kindergarteners and handicapped children, cooperative and vocational education?

- What is the teaching and administration like?

- What is the average class size and teacher-pupil ratio?

- What provisions are there for textbooks, school bus service, hot lunch programs, and extracurricular activities?

School Records

The sooner the child's present school information is obtained and transferred, the sooner he can begin adjusting to the new school and avoid misplacement. So arrange time with your child's present teacher to review the youngster's progress and school records, making sure to have a copy of his vital information forwarded to his new school at least a month before the scheduled move.

If records can't be sent until grades are posted at the time of the child's withdrawal, go by the school the day the child checks out to get copies of all school records. Have a manila envelope with the child's name clearly indicated on it and include in it copies of:

- His birth certificate.

- His medical, dental, and orthodontic records.

- His immunization records.

- A list of the textbooks he has used.

- A description of the grading method used by his former teacher.

- A statement from his teacher indicating the student's current level of achievement, interests, and any special programs he has been involved in.

Don't wait to have the new school request your child's school records. This can delay his placement in the right grade or classes. Take the records with you.

For an older child, call ahead to the new school and ask what is needed for sports eligibility and when athletic try-outs are scheduled. (Then, if possible, you can time the move so that the child can be involved in his favorite sport, which is a good way to meet and become associated with other children of similar interests.)

Most schools require that a transfer student present a letter from a doctor certifying that the student has had a physical examination within the past twelve months. If your child has already had a physician's check-up for camp or sports, take a copy of the letter with you to save him several weeks of delay before being declared eligible to participate in athletic activities.

Saying Goodbye

Provide an address book and let your child collect the addresses and phone numbers of his friends. Allow him to exchange photos with them. He can make his own "change of address" cards (decorated with stickers) to give to friends before leaving. He can also be allowed to invite a few friends over for dinner or an outing before your final departure.

As the Girl Scout songs goes, "Make new friends, but keep the old; one is silver, and the other gold." You can foster continuity by helping your child keep in touch with a few "best friends" back home. Provide stationery for him and encourage him to correspond regularly with friends, grandparents, or cousins. Besides being a great boost to writing skills, corresponding with "golden" friends provides a sense of roots and connection. Perhaps a visit between old friends or close relatives of his age can be arranged.

At the New School

Support from family and school is important in smoothing a school transfer and building a bridge of communication. At the first opportunity, go and meet your child's new teacher. Often the more welcoming the school is, the better the new child's adjustment.

Chisholm Elementary School in Edmond, Oklahoma, gives a special party for new students at the beginning of the year. They also have an evening party and informal meeting for the parents of new students. Newcomers are introduced by placing their pictures on the entry wall at the weekly all-school opening. The faculty and staff go out of their way to welcome new arrivals. Ryan's family had moved every two years before coming to Edmond. His mother says that this move has been his best adjustment so far, largely due to the warm reception given new students at Chisholm.

Many schools assign a peer helper or "buddy" for the new student to show him around and help him find the cafeteria, library, and classrooms during the first few difficult and confusing days. One family found pen pals for their children before the move (they wrote ahead and got the names of students of similar ages and interests). After corresponding for a few months, the children's budding friendships provided a great support when they arrived at their new school.

Keep in close touch with the new school counselor or reading specialist who handles the testing and placement of transfer students. It also helps to visit the classroom and spend a half-day watching it in action. Know what's being taught and what the new teacher expects. Find out what books will be read and how much homework is assigned. You can also share information that can help your child's teacher understand him quicker and better.

If your child has special academic needs, don't leave it to time or chance for the teacher to discover them. Meet with the school principal to go over the child's records and discuss your observations in order to determine how the new school can best help your child to make the adjustment.

There is some evidence to suggest a link between frequent school moves and an increased risk of school drop-out, according to Dr. Carol Kelly. "Families and schools must work closely together to find ways to maximize success for new students," she says.

Be aware of tracking procedures in the new school (assignment to low, average, and honors classes). Sara, who moved to a school in another state, was placed in the lowest level math group due to overcrowding in the class where she really belonged. She was bored and began to lose confidence and enthusiasm because she was in a group that was a full year behind her regular math class. After the third week, her parents had a conference with Sara's teacher and asked for reassessment of her math aptitude and a transfer to a class that would fit her ability.

What Enrichment Is Offered?

Our daughter had been in the new school in Maine three months before we discovered that chorus, band, bells, recorder ensemble, and other enrichment programs were available within the school day (for several of these activities, the students arrived at 7:30 a.m.). So ask what enrichment opportunities are offered in your child's new school!

If the child already has a strong interest in a particular sport or activity — dance, gymnastics, tennis, art, or some other program — encourage him to be involved in it at the new school or to continue lessons outside of class. This interest will help smooth the moving process as he meets other youngsters with whom he has a common interest, rather than being isolated in a strange new environment. (This is especially important if the child is shy). A talent or sports skill boosts self-esteem and provides a way to become known and recognized in the new setting.

Emily, a sixteen-year-old who moved from Washington to Connecticut during the middle of her junior year (usually a difficult time), played the piano and flute. By participating in the high school band, she quickly made new friends, which smoothed her transition considerably.

Get Involved

Volunteer to help at school and join the parent-teacher association. You will meet other parents with common interests, get to know teachers and students, and learn what is going on in the educational programs of the new school.

Listening and Accepting

Being present and available when her children arrived home from school was of foremost importance in their adjustment after moving, said Janie, a mother of three. They talked about their day, vented some frustrations and negative feelings (like their embarrassment about being made fun of because of their Southern accents), had a snack, and then went to do homework or shoot baskets.

Most people who move go through some form of the grieving process, and children are no exception. Some are born with an ability to easily handle the stress of moving; they are friendlier and more adaptable to change. Others are more sensitive, shy, and take longer to adjust to a new situation.

The impact which mobility has upon children also varies with their age. Under age four, most children haven't developed binding social ties outside the family. Nine- and ten-year-olds have strong friendships, and often it takes longer for them to let go of their loyalty to past friends and make new ones. Teenagers who move face possible problems of loneliness and shaken identity.

The speed at which adjustment takes place is different for each child, but the following are representative of the usual stages involved in the transition process:

Denial: "This isn't happening. I'm not going. I'll stay with friends and go to school here!"

Anger: "Why me? Why did Dad have to take that promotion and move me to this boring little town?"

Acceptance/ "Here I am. Maybe I can do here
Adjustment: what I did back home. I think I'll go out for basketball and join the Spanish Club.

"It's okay for kids to mourn their past life and loss of friends," says Priscilla, who moved her four children to Maine from Idaho. "We should allow them to say what they miss about the old school and what they don't like about the new situation, and accept and support them in that. Rather than trying to gloss over negative feelings, we need a balance."

"Don't expect instant adjustment," says Joan, a mom who moved her six children from the East Coast to California.

Confused, excited, happy, sad — whatever their reaction — we can help our young people adjust by not squashing or denying their feelings.

If our children stay angry or depressed for an extended time (which can drain their motivation and rob them of the energy they need for school work), they need extra support. By listening, by being positive and hopeful, and by getting additional assistance when needed from the school counselor or a trusted pastor, we can help our children make a positive adjustment to moving and keep on learning in their new school setting.

Two Students

Jeremy

Jeremy is thirteen years old and has moved to seven different schools in the past three years. Here are some of his observations about moving:

"It's scary at a new school until I make friends, and sometimes that takes weeks. If you don't know anyone, you're usually left out. You feel real down when everyone is playing sports at recess and you're just sitting there. If you get in with the wrong crowd, then you're stuck there. The teachers tell the nerds to be nice to you.

"It's hard to get involved in sports because the kids don't think new kids are any good and don't want you to play. If you're really good at a sport or something, then they accept you more. At most of the schools, kids have not been friendly at all. You have to earn their friendships. I did start to know a few boys better in soccer season.

"I have a lot of catching up to do, especially in English. Last year at my school in Tacoma, we didn't do anything in English. I turned in a paper half right and got an A+. So I felt behind from the first in my new junior high, which is harder."

John

John has made three school changes since kindergarten, but at age fourteen he faced his first cross-country move. He arrived in his new location right at the beginning of basketball season and tried out the first week. He is good at the sport and really cares about it, which helped him to get to know other boys in the new junior high. He met a boy on the basketball team and they eventually became "best friends." John qualified for honors classes and his grades stayed high, but his adjustment was not without some difficulties, as he explains:

"Usually new kids are made fun of for anything different. The first day I walked into science class, the whole class laughed. They had passed around the news that I was going to have rolled-up pants and a skateboarder's haircut. They all wore jeans and T-shirts. I did have on khaki pants (acceptable in our old school), my brother's, rolled up a little at the bottom because mine were still packed in a box — and I was the laughingstock that day."

Here is the advice Jeremy and John give to children who are moving to a new school:

- "Don't be fake or imitate someone else; be yourself."
- "Get involved with a sport, extracurricular activity, club or something you're good at and enjoy. You'll develop friendships because you're doing something together."
- "Be patient, although that's hard sometimes."

Suggested Reading on Moving

Reading about other children's experiences with moving may be helpful to your child and open up discussion. Here are some books on the subject which can be checked out from your local library:

For children ages five and up:

- *Aldo Applesauce* by J. Hurwitz
- *Gloomy Louie* by P. Green
- *I'm Moving* by Martha Hickman
- *Janey* by Charlotte Zolotow
- *Maggie and the Goodbye Gift* by Sue and Jerry Milord
- *Mitchell Is Moving* by Marjorie Sharmat
- *Pip Moves Away* by M.B. Brown

For 'tweens:

- *Between Friends* by Sheila Garrigue
- *Anything for a Friend* by Ellen Conford
- *Anastasia Again!* by Lois Lowry

For teens:

- *The Teenager's Survival Guide to Moving* by P.C. Nida and W.M. Heller
- *Help! We're Moving* by Dianna Daniels Booher

Chapter 18

DOUBLE-BARRELED HELP FOR SINGLE-PARENT KIDS!

I listened as my new neighbor Carol poured out her story. After a divorce, she had been left with a demanding job and was trying to get her two boys adjusted in a new school. Now, back at work, she had been called by the school counselor. John, a second-grader, was having problems learning to read and was falling behind in class. Aaron, the seventh-grader, had tested low in math and language and needed further evaluation.

My heart went out to Carol as I recalled my mother, widowed at thirty-six with six children, and the difficulties she faced that first year as a single parent.

Carol is not alone, for ninety percent of all single-parent homes are headed by females. Most recent studies indicate 26.3 percent of households with children under 18 are headed by a single parent. Research shows that children from single-parent homes consistently score lower on achievement tests and make lower grades in school than children from two-parent homes.[1]

What Causes This Low Achievement?

Educators say that the negative factors which contribute to low achievement include emotional stress, lack of parental involvement in the educational process, a child's sex (boys seem to be more affected by divorce than girls), and lowered expectations by both teacher and parent.[2]

Most single parents are juggling the demands of a full-time job, household, and child care all alone. How can they provide a foundation for achievement in their children's lives?

A Background for Achievement

Many single parents are doing a great job of encouraging learning and achievement.

For example, there is Sonia Carson, a single mother. Although she worked three jobs in inner-city Detroit to feed her family, she took them to church weekly where her son Benjamin caught a vision of becoming a missionary doctor. At school, however, Benjamin was at the bottom of his class and in the lowest reading group. One cause of his problems was poor eyesight. His school work improved once he had been fitted with correctly prescribed eyeglasses, but a bigger problem was his lack of motivation. His mother cut her sons' television viewing down to three pre-selected shows a week. Both boys were required to read two library books a week, in addition to completing their homework assignments.

Within eighteen months Benjamin went from last to first place in his class and stayed there all through high school, where he received a full scholarship to Yale University. From there he went on to graduate from the University of Michigan Medical School and is now chief of pediatric neurosurgery at Johns Hopkins Hospital in Baltimore. Dr. Benjamin Carson, for the first time in medical history, successfully separated head-joined Siamese twins. In addition to being a respected brain surgeon, he is also a committed Christian who acknowledges God's guidance in his operation procedures and techniques, and who takes time to encourage ghetto youth.

Then there is Dixie's son. Kyle is a single-parent child who derives a lot of confidence from being able to help his mother try new tasks, and take initiative.

"We've got to change this tire; we'll figure it out together," is his attitude when the tire on their small car goes flat. His mother has taught him to put oil in the car. He helps with the household chores, like keeping his room clean, vacuuming the house, and cleaning out the garage. He feels that he is a needed and worthwhile part of the family.

But Kyle is not burdened down with too many responsibilities. He has free time to play soccer and baseball, enjoy friends and attend church functions. Being a capable kid carries over into his school activities. His teachers say that he is very responsible, mature, and willing to help other students. Kyle and his mom Dixie spend special times together and do a lot of talking to each other.

Single-parenting is a tremendous challenge, but let's look at some suggestions single-parent families have shared with me that help to provide a background for learning and success for the single-parent child.

241

1. Provide effective communication and emotional support for the child.

Communication

The emotional turmoil that surrounds a divorce, death, or family crisis can block much of the information presented at school and stall or even reverse a child's academic progress. Helping her learn to handle stress is crucial. Lines of communication between the parent and child must be kept open.

There needs to be time to talk and listen in a non-judgmental way, an opportunity for the child to express her feelings and thoughts without restraint or fear of a negative reaction. There should be time to talk about what happened during the day, what she is doing in school and extra-curricular activities, what she is learning and interested in. Besides lessening emotional stress, conversation stimulates thinking, language, and listening skills, all vital tools for school success. It also offers the child a chance to sift through the facts and ideas presented at school.

Sometimes opportunities for communication will crop up while you and your child are doing something together — cooking, raking leaves, or doing dishes. Dinnertime and bedtime are prime opportunities for sharing. "One of the most helpful times for my family was a one-on-one breakfast hour to keep in touch with where they were and where they wanted to go," says a single mother of three teenagers.

"We tried to have straight communication every morning and evening to avoid surprises," said Allen, a single parent of two girls. "Like a quarterback directing a team, I'd say, 'You're going to be at piano at 3:15, and you'll be at Suzie's. I'll be home at five o'clock. Are we all squared away on this?' Then we also gathered at dinner. I don't allow straggling meals where one eats and later another eats in front of the TV. I feel convergence around the table, saying grace, having a sense of order is important."

It is also important to provide a strong support network.

An Emotional Support Network

Providing a support network system with a caring neighbor, close family friends and relatives, a grandparent or teacher is also helpful. Other adults in the child's life can contribute much to emotional stability.

"My grandparents provided a very strong, positive relationship. We did things together like fishing, taking long walks, sewing, and reading," says Carol Vicary, whose parents were divorced when she was very young. "Mother worked full-time while struggling with multiple sclerosis. My mom's cousin spent time with me; she took me shopping, to movies and plays. She taught me about fashion and etiquette. From birth to age seven, I had the same babysitter whose home was out in the country. There I acquired a love for flowers, animals, and the outdoors. Ministers, youth workers, and Young Life leaders also added a lot of stability in crucial times of my life." Carol, now married and the mother of a son, had an excellent record of achievement in high school and college.

After her husband and daughter died in a car accident, Ellene felt almost overwhelmed with the responsibility of raising her son. She enrolled Jeremy in a Christian school for his seventh-grade year.

"Right away Jeremy began playing on the school's football team and benefitting from good relationships with the coaches. He also had a principal and a whole staff of teachers who cared about him personally. He gained friends from homes that shared the same values as ours. There Jeremy has found a 'niche' in this big world where he is accepted and can excel in positive ways. This is a big support encouragement to me."

In addition to his mother, other dads have been good role-models for Jeremy and have filled some of his emotional needs. One family friend called and invited him to go with him and his son on a National Guard weekend bivouac in the field, a military experience Jeremy will never forget. His soccer coach became a close friend and invited Jeremy to his home often to learn to play computer games with his son and to share their acreage and their love. The family pastor took Jeremy to play golf with him. Times like these have made a tremendous difference in Jeremy's life.

Ellene and Jeremy have a special family night once a week. They go out to eat and talk, or to play games together.

Warning Signs

Many children act out their inner feelings, and we need to read signals of behavior. Withdrawal, excessive sadness and "crying jags," failing grades, hostility, and aggression indicate unresolved problems lurking underneath the surface and may call for extra help.

"After my husband left, Jennifer, eight years old, seemed so helpful with the three-year-old," says Gail, a secretary and single parent. "I was having a difficult time, feeling sorry for myself, depressed, trying to get our life together. After two months of school, the teacher called me and told me that Jennifer was a very angry girl. She took her anger out on everyone and everything at school. The teacher felt she needed help, and recommended the school counselor. What I learned is that we forget sometimes that our children suffer through losses just like we do, and because they want to protect their moms, they try to be big and not show they are hurting too. Be sure to be aware of your children's emotions and what they go through."

Parents should not be shy about getting the necessary support they may need from pastor, counselor, family, or friends. As the family re-establishes stability and the child is helped with her emotions, she can be set free to concentrate on her studies at school.

2. Recognize the impact of role-modeling on learning.

The number one way a single parent can provide a background for achievement is through *role-modeling,* says Dr. William Shreeve, chairman of the Department of Education, Eastern Washington State University. Parents often don't realize the powerful effect of their role-modeling. This is important for every child, but especially for single-parent kids. The more the child sees the parent as a reader, writer, and learner, the more positive she will be toward learning.

When there are books, magazines, and newspapers in the home, when parents read aloud to and with their children, when the family spends time discussing newspaper articles, special interests, and favorite books — then good role-modeling is taking place. Letting your child see you write a letter of thanks to a business or a friend models the value of writing. (At the same time you can give the child some note paper on which to write a relative who has agreed to correspond. You can also model writing for your child by putting up a chalkboard on which you leave notes like: "I'll be home at five o'clock." "I like the way you cleaned your room." "Don't forget to start your homework!")

Share your hobbies with your child, and continue to pursue your own special interests. "I enrolled in a community college to begin stretching my mind in the academic area; when I went back to school, we all did our homework together in the evening," said one single mother.

Family activities like cooking from a recipe and playing board games boosts your child's skill development in reading, problem-solving, and following directions.

Mary, a teacher and a single parent, suggests that one way to encourage writing and provide emotional support for the child is to have her write to both sets of grandparents. This activity helps the child to understand: "Yes, your parents are separated, but you haven't lost your grandparents; I'll help you keep this relationship going." The child can send school papers, stories, and art work to her grandparents, and they can write back — extending support for the child and giving her a reason to write and learn.

3. Establish a regular family schedule and closely regulate homework and TV time.

Parent apathy toward homework, say teachers, transfers to low achievement in children. Parents can reinforce good study habits by organizing a space and time for homework, and by guarding against overscheduling. A quiet place, writing supplies, a dictionary, and other reference materials are needed. Organization is a vital ingredient in the learning process.

"That first fall the girls and I were alone together, it hit me that we had a homework problem," said Allen. "Neither daughter wanted to study. One was totally disorganized, losing papers and waiting until the night before a big project was due to announce it. We talked about what a good assignment notebook looks like, and I had the girls keep it up daily and plan ahead on projects. I put some of my evening meetings aside to spend more time with the girls. Their spelling was very weak, so I'd ask early in the week, 'What are your spelling words? Let's put them on the refrigerator and go over them.' And we saw grades come way up for the term."

Children thrive on order and structure. Allen shared how important it was in his case to re-establish a family routine. Guidelines for family behavior and a regular schedule for eating, sleeping, playing, and studying aid learning.

When there is a test, perhaps you can help your child by asking her questions about the material. This kind of study and review can actually be fun for both of you: for the child, because you're doing it together; for you, because you're discovering how your child learns. You can even make a game out of reviewing information. Fifteen minutes of oral practice can often make the difference between an A and a C.

During the week, television viewing needs to be limited. "On school nights, we don't watch television," says Judy Meyer, an accountant and a single parent. "During the week we tape favorite shows and view them on the weekend when time is not so short. I supervise the completion of the homework, take Brian to art and karate lessons, and save time to play with and read to him. On the weekends that Brian is with me, we usually have one of his friends over to spend the night and do some special activity. Brian is also given some chores and responsibilities around the house, including a pet to care for. We do all our own housecleaning and yard work together, giving him a sense of home life." Setting some time aside to just have fun together — taking a trip to the zoo, going on a picnic in the park, anything both enjoy — they found, is important even with all the responsibilities.

After-school matters

Younger children especially need supervision after school. You might consider looking into a high-quality after-school care program at a neighbor's house or at your child's school, YMCA, or local church where recreation, a snack, and homework help are available. If the child is old enough to stay home alone until you return from work, a college student or retired teacher could provide some after-school homework help or accompany the child to the library for material for research reports or to help her choose books to check out for independent reading at home.

If the child gets "stuck" with a problem in math or a difficult sentence in writing, Homework Hot-Line or Dial-a-Teacher can provide help over the phone. (Many cities have such programs for students; ask your school or local college for the telephone numbers in your area.)

Parental Involvement and Expectations

There is a strong correlation between parental involvement and school achievement, and teacher expectations of a child from a single-parent home are often lower than for those from traditional two-parent environments. One key to overcoming this situation is to go in to meet the teacher at the first of the year. Let her *know* that you are interested in seeing your child get a quality education. Let her know that you will help at home if needed (this show of concern and willingness to become involved communicates care and support for education).

"When the parent comes in and presents herself as an active learner, bright, showing interest and support for the school, there is an automatic upping of communication and expectations that makes the child's education better," says Kerry Jones, reading specialist in the Yarmouth, Maine, schools. "Learning becomes a shared responsibility and the child, parent, and teacher can feel it. Supportive parents seen in school can make a better place for their child."

Written communication with the teacher can develop rapport without taking the parent away from his job. "You wouldn't believe the effect of a positive note from a parent. In a class of twenty-five children, the teacher gets very few positive notes all year, like: 'My child is really happy in school; you must be doing something right,' or 'I've never seen Jennifer so eager to learn — she's always reading.' It only takes a few minutes and doesn't take the parent away from the job, but it can make all the difference in building cooperation," adds Ms. Jones.

Parental expectations are also important. We can continue to have high hopes for our children and their future, encouraging but not pressuring. "We shouldn't use the divorce as an excuse to lower expectations," a single parent says. Instead, discover and build on your child's strengths: talents in music, art, or sports; budding skills in horseback riding or woodworking; special interests and hobbies; strong character traits like faith, compassion, or loyalty. Highlight the positives at home and school and help your child find ways to compensate and learn what is needed through her own learning style. Appreciate what she does well even if it is small. Building self-esteem and an "I can do it" attitude will carry over to more progress at school.

In addition, research shows that parent attendance at school events is associated with higher student grades. "Take as active a role as possible in whatever activities your child is interested in, especially when he gets into junior and senior high school. Try to attend, if he has a debate, drama, athletic event, whatever. Your youngsters may never say, 'I appreciate your being here,' but *they always look for you!"* says Dr. Shreeve.

Schools all over the country are coming up with ways to arrange conferences, performances, and parent meetings to suit the demanding schedules of single and working parents:

- Holding parent-teacher conferences early in the morning, in the evening, or on weekends. In Austin, Texas, some teachers even make house calls.

- Scheduling breakfast, supper, or Saturday PTA meetings with babysitters or movies provided to keep children entertained while their parents attend meetings.

- Providing copies of video tapes of school presentations for a small fee, so when parents cannot attend, they can share the performance later together at home.

- Establishing classroom parent centers where parents can visit, observe classroom teaching and interaction, and check out books and materials, such as skill sheets, games, and activities for use at home.

In addition, many schools are providing volunteer opportunities for parents. When time and work schedules permit, parents can share hobbies, travel experiences, and other interesting bits of information that complement classroom units. Participating in a Saturday Bike Safety Day or school carnival, or serving as a cafeteria volunteer once a month (and having a chance to eat lunch with the child) are both good opportunities for active involvement.

Emotional support and communication, positive role-modeling, supervision of homework and television viewing, participation with the school, and positive contacts with teachers — with these ingredients, children in single-parent families can do far more than just survive their school years. They can *achieve* and grow in skills and confidence to tackle all the challenges which lie ahead.

CHILDREN LEARN
WHAT THEY LIVE

Dorothy Law Nolte's poem, "Children Learn What They Live," tells us how children develop values of justice, honesty, compassion, confidence, and faith. Just as surely, kids also develop attitudes about learning — attitudes we have talked about in this book, attitudes we can encourage that children often carry for a lifetime:

If a child lives with books, storytelling, and reading aloud on his parents' laps, he learns to enjoy reading.

If a child lives with notes and letters exchanged in the course of his family life, he learns to enjoy writing.

If a child has conversation with parents and siblings around the dinner table, and while working and playing together, he learns good language and listening skills.

If a child has time and encouragement to develop his own plans and carry out projects, he learns initiative.

If a child learns to finish jobs at home and to get his school work and homework done readily, he learns responsibility and task-commitment.

If a child is taught to be organized with his books and possessions at home, he learns to be reliable with the hundreds of handouts, tests and materials that cross his desk at school. If a child's learning style and strengths are discovered and respected, he becomes an active learner and grows in confidence and self-esteem.

If a child's questions are encouraged, his curiosity flourishes and he has a sense of wonder about the world.

If a child has stability and security at home, he has inner stability and can focus and concentrate on his studies and achieve in school tasks.

If a child lives with positive expectations and has success in meeting them, he gains motivation for the challenges ahead.

Our homes can be the place where we find delight in just who and where our kids are at each stage of development, a place where they can develop the spark inside — the motivation — to find joy in learning and someday realize their "Great Expectations"!

Appendix A

WRITING BOOSTERS

Preschoolers and Kindergarteners:

Help your kids make their own books. Take dictation and turn your child's stories into books. Covers can be made of cardboard or construction paper, and pages can be sewn or stapled. For an "All About Me" book, your child might choose ten pictures from infancy to the present, put them in chronological order and glue them into the scrapbook. Suggest he dictate to you what is happening in each picture or write it in invented spelling.

Give writing props to go along with fantasy play. Pretend play is a wonderful way for youngsters to explore their own creativity. If you place clipboards, order pads, envelopes, paper and pencil near their costumes and props, kids frequently will incorporate them into the fantasy, whether they are playing hospital, restaurant or office.

Write "lunch box love notes" and other messages to your kids. Children love to receive notes in their lunch boxes or on their desks. Even if they are too young to read very well, they will work to figure out the message — "I love you! Have a happy day!" — and send one back.

First to Third Graders:

Let children create a treasure hunt for friends, siblings or even parents. The child writes clues on slips of paper for the hunter. "Your next clue is in the living room by something red." "Beside the birdhouse is your treat."

Compile lots of lists. Provide youngsters with little notepads or rolls of adding-machine tape, and let them make list upon list. Some suggestions: favorite friends, favorite books, places they've been, daily chores, supplies for picnics or trips.

Make original greeting cards. Have your child create birthday, Valentine or holiday cards and write his own greeting or poem. Supply construction paper. These can be decorated with stickers, cut-out pictures or original illustrations.

Encourage letter-writing. After Christmas and birthdays, thank-you notes are in order. On vacation, kids choose postcards to send to friends, family and favorite teachers. At home, supply bright stationery, envelopes and stamps in a basket and get a correspondence going between a relative and your child.

Fourth Through Sixth Graders:

Encourage journal keeping. Besides being excellent writing practice, a journal is a great outlet for expressing feelings and ideas. Provide a blank book and suggest your child fill it with what happens at school and home, events on trips, hopes and dreams, poems and opinions.

Rainy Day Writing. Put titles for stories on slips of paper in a paper bag, and include a small pad of paper and pencil inside. Your child can write stories about his activities, friends, or just-for-fun made up stories.

Pick a pen pal. As a result of correspondence with a foreign friend, your child gets insights into how people in other cultures live. Send a self-addressed, stamped envelope to: International Friendship League, Department A, 55 Mt. Vernon St., Boston, MA 02108.

Most important, praise your child's writing. Respond as a sensitive, caring reader rather than a critic who focuses on errors. Show interest and appreciation by keeping stories in a folder after they have been displayed. There are lots of opportunities in family life for mutual sharing and support for writing, two key ingredients for your child to become a fluent writer.

For many creative ways to help your child *enjoy* writing and improve writing and reading skills, see Cheri's book *HOMELIFE: The Key to Your Child's Success at School.*

Appendix B

MATH BOOSTERS

Preschoolers and Kindergarteners:

Children learn best from hands-on activities in which they use math for real reasons in the course of their day like *sorting* laundry, blocks, silverware to put away; *cooking,* where they learn about measuring, temperature, time, and dividing portions; and *comparing:* "Which apple is bigger?"

Puzzles and blocks. Puzzles give practice in identifying shapes and matching colors. While playing with blocks, children also learn math concepts like weight, size, spatial relationships and order.

Singing number songs and fingerplay. "Five Frogs Sitting on a Log," "Ten Little Indians," "Five Little Pumpkins," "Ten Bears in Bed." Jump rope counting games also provide good practice in counting.

First to Third Graders:

Games for building math skills. Board games like Chutes and Ladders, Bingo, and Presto-Change-O develop math skills. Card games like Old Maid, Go Fish, Crazy Eights, or Hearts provide practice in counting, categorizing, reasoning and strategy. Also dominoes, bowling and computer games can build skills for math.

Memorizing with Style. Consider your child's learning strengths when you help him master math facts. Using a tape recorder along with flashcards helps some children. Practicing multiplication tables while bouncing a ball or shooting baskets helps active learners as we saw, and setting the addition and subtraction facts to music works best for some kids.

Lemonade or cookie stand. Let your child have a toy sale or help you with a garage sale, set up a lemonade or cookie stand for some real practice in pricing and handling money.

Mental Math. A good exercise for kids while you're riding in the car together, is to ask your child a continuous problem to be figured in his head, like 2 divided by 5 times 6 minus three equals ?

Fourth to Sixth Graders:

Grocery Store Math. Let your child clip coupons and help you figure savings at the grocery store. If you see a half-price sale, have your child help you figure the prices. If bananas are three pounds for a dollar, ask him to figure how much it will cost to buy one pound, two pounds or five pounds.

Setting up a budget. Your child can have a goal (the purchase of a certain toy), find out how much money it will take to reach that goal, and how much weekly allowance he can save.

Math puzzles that come in paperback books are enjoyable and challenging ways to practice math skills.

For more ideas on ways to boost motivation for math, see HOME-LIFE.

NOTES

Chapter 1

[1] *Webster's New World Dictionary of the American Language* (New York: Warner Books, 1984), p. 393.

Chapter 2

[1] From an interview with Dr. Arthur Bodin, past president of the Division of Family Psychology of the American Psychological Association, who now practices in Palo Alto, California, where he is also a senior research fellow at the Mental Research Institute.

[2] Dorothy Corkille Briggs, *Your Child's Self-Esteem* (New York: Doubleday, 1970), p. 3.

[3] From an interview with Mrs. Edith Schaeffer.

[4] Ross Campbell, *How To Really Love Your Teenager* (Wheaton, Illinois: Victor Books, 1981), p. 31.

[5] Briggs, p. 68.

Chapter 3

[1] *Who Will Be My Teacher?* (Waco: Word Books, 1985), p. 23.

[2] Jim Trelease, *The Read-Aloud Handbook* (New York: Viking Penguin Inc., 1985), p. 20.

[3] *Essays into Literacy* (Portsmouth: Heinnemann Educational Books, 1983), p. 100.

[4] Proverbs 12:24 *Good News Bible*.

Chapter 4

[1] The material in this chapter first appeared in *FAMILY CIRCLE*, September 5, 1989, and is used by permission.

[2] *NEA Today*, Nov. 1988, p. 5.

[3]Dr. Darrel Lang and Bill Stinson, *Lazy Dogs and Snoozing Frogs* (LaCrosse, Wisconsin: Coulee Press, 1988), p. 5.

[4]Ibid., p. 5.

[5](New York: Alfred A. Knopf, 1987).

[6](Denver: Accent Books, 1988), p. 100.

Chapter 5

[1]Proverbs 22:6 NAS.

[2]*According to Dr. H. William Mitchell, quoted in* HOMEMADE, Vol. 22, No. 11, November 1988, published by *Family Concern.*

[3]Proverbs 17:9 TLB.

[4]*Your Child's Self-Esteem* (New York: Doubleday, 1975), p. 272.

Chapter 6

[1]Miriam Adderholdt-Elliott, "What's Bad About Being Good?" *The Education Digest,* Nov. 1988, p. 27.

Chapter 7

[1]*Parents and Teenagers Newsletter,* Vol. 1, No. 1, Thomas Schultz Publications, Inc., p. 1.

[2]*Time,* May 1988.

[3]*Parents and Teenagers Newsletter,* p. 1.

[4](Old Tappan: Fleming H. Revell Company, 1975).

Chapter 8

[1]*Don't Push Your Preschooler* (New York: Harper & Row, 1980), p. 203.

[2]Ibid., pp. 201-203.

[3]Ibid., p. 8.

[4]Ibid.

[5]*The Book of Unusual Quotations,* Rudolf Flesch, Ed. (New York: Harper & Row, 1957), p. 204.

[6](New York: Prentice Hall Books for Young Readers/A Division of Simon & Schuster, Inc. New York.)

[7]Ibid.

[8]*In Their Own Way* (Los Angeles: Jeremy T. Tarcher, Inc., 1987), p. 141.

Chapter 9

[1]In his book, HIDE OR SEEK (Old Tappan: Fleming H. Revell, 1974), Dr. James Dobson writes more about helping children compensate and develop high self-esteem.

[2]*Frames of Mind: The Theory of Multiple Intelligences* (New York: Basic Books Inc., 1983).

Chapter 10

[1]*Raising Self-Reliant Children in a Self-Indulgent World* (Rocklin, CA: Prima Publishing, 1989).

²Ibid., p. 28.

³*Your Child's Self-Esteem* (New York: Doubleday, 1975), p. 273.

⁴"Habits of the Hearth," *Christianity Today*, Feb. 3, 1989, p. 24.

⁵Ibid.

⁶Frank B. Gilbreath, Jr., and Ernestine Gilbreath Carey (New York: Bantam Books, 1963).

⁷From an excerpt from *Papa, My Father* (New York: Slack, Inc., 1989) as quoted in *Reader's Digest,* Sept. 1989, p. 79.

⁸Ibid., p 80.

⁹Ibid.

¹⁰(New York: E.P. Dutton, 1987).

¹¹Ibid, p. 95.

¹²Raymond S. Moore, *Bulletin Num. 62,* the Moore Foundation, Box 12, Camas, WA 98607.

¹³Priscilla Vail, *Smart Kids with School Problems* (New York: E.P. Dutton, 1987), p. 164.

¹⁴130 Cremona, Box 1911, Santa Barbara, CA 93116-1911.

Chapter 11

¹Published by Cherry Lane Music Company, Port Chester, New York.

²*Newsweek*, Sept. 7, 1987, p. 60.

³*What Works: Research About Teaching and Learning,* United States Department of Education, William J. Bennett, Secretary, 1986, p. 25.

⁴Vance Packard, *A Nation of Strangers* (New York: David McKay, Inc., 1972).

⁵*The Story Song,* Marcia Lane © 1982, The Enchanted Loom Story Company, 462 Amsterdam Avenue, New York, NY 10024.

⁶William Zimmerman, *Instant Oral Biographies* (New York: Guarionex Press, Ltd., 1982).

Chapter 12

¹*Time*, Sept. 11, 1989, p. 68.

²Ibid.

³"Helping Kids Like the Lab," *Newsweek*, Feb. 15, 1988, pp. 58,59.

⁴*MISEDUCATION: Preschoolers at Risk* (New York: Alfred A. Knopf, 1987), p. 119.

⁵*Your Child's Self-Esteem* (New York: Doubleday, 1975), pp. 264,265.

⁶(New York: Addison Wesley Publishing Company, Inc., 1989).

⁷*The Normal Child and Primary Education* (Massachusetts: Silver, Burdett & Ginn, Inc., 1912, 1940).

Chapter 13

¹(Cambridge: Harvard University Press, 1984), p. 9.

Chapter 18

[1] William Shreeve, William G.J. Goetter and Adrian Bunn, "Single Parents and Student Achievement," *USA Today*, July 1986, p. 58.

[2] Ibid.

BIBLIOGRAPHY

Adderholdt-Elliott, Miriam. "What's Bad About Being Good?" *The Education Digest*, Nov. 1988.

Ames, Louise Bates and Ames, Joan Chase. *Don't Push Your Preschooler*. New York: Harper & Row, 1980.

Armstrong, Thomas Dr. *In Their Own Way*. Los Angeles: Jeremy T. Tarcher, Inc., 1987.

Bettleheim, Bruno. *A Good Enough Parent*. New York: Alfred A. Knoff, 1987.

Briggs, Dorothy Corkille. *Your Child's Self-Esteem*. New York: Doubleday, 1975.

Burron, Arnold. Children & Stress. Denver: Accent Books, 1988.

Cambell, Ross. *How to Really Love Your Teenager*. Wheaton, Illinois: Victor Books, 1981.

Dobson, James Dr. *Dare To Discipline*. Wheaton: Tyndale, 1970.

Dobson, James Dr. HIDE OR SEEK. Old Tappan: Fleming H. Revell, 1974.

Dobson, James Dr. *Parenting Isn't for Cowards*. Dallas: Word, 1987.

Elkind, David. *MISEDUCATION: Preschoolers at Risk*. New York: Alfred A. Knoff, 1987.

FAMILY CIRCLE, Sept. 1989.

Fuller, Cheri. HOME-LIFE: Preparing Your Child For *Success At School*. Tulsa: Honor Books, 1988.

Gardner, Howard Dr. *Frames of Mind: The Theory of Multiple Intelligences*. New York: Basic Books, Inc., 1983.

Gartlett, Marti. *Who Will Be My Teacher?* Waco: Word Books, 1985.

Gesell, Arnold Dr. *The Normal Child and Primary Education.* Massachusetts: Silver, Burdett & Ginn Inc., 1912, 1940.

Gilbreath, Frank B., Jr. and Carey, Ernestine Gilbreath. *Cheaper By the Dozen.* New York: Bantam Books, 1963.

"Habits of the Hearth," *Christianity Today,* Feb. 3, 1989.

"Helping Kids Like the Lab," *Newsweek,* Feb. 15, 1988.

Holt, John. *Learning All the Time.* New York: Addison Wesley Publishing Company, Inc., 1989.

HOMEMADE, Vol. 22, No. 11, Nov. 1988.

Kraus, Leo. *Leo the Late Bloomer.* Used by permission of the Publisher, Prentice-Hall Books for Young Readers / A Division of Simon & Schuster, Inc. New York, 1971.

Lang, Darrel Dr. and Stinson, Bill. *Lazy Dogs and Snoozing Frogs.* LaCrosse, Wisconsin: Coulee Press, 1988.

Lewis, C.S. *Shared Treasures.*

Moore, Raymond S. *Bulletin Num. 62,* the Moore Foundation.

NEA Today, Nov. 1988.

Newsweek, Sept. 7, 1987.

Packard, Vance. *A Nation of Strangers.* New York: David McKay, Inc., 1972.

Parents and Teenagers Newsletter, Vol. 1, No. 1, Thomas Schultz Publications, Inc.

Reader's Digest, Sept. 1989.

Schaeffer, Edith. *What Is a Family?* Old Tappan: Fleming H. Revell Company, 1975.

Shreeve, William, Goetter, William G.J. and Bunn, Adrian. "Single Parents and Student Achievement," *USA Today,* July 1986.

Smith, Frank. *Essays into Literacy.* Portsmouth: Heinnemann Educational Books, 1983.

Stephen, Glenn H. *Raising Self-Reliant Children in a Self-Indulgent World.* Rocklin, CA: Prima Publishing, 1989.

Time, May 1988.

Time, Sept. 11, 1989.

The Book of Unusual Quotations, Rudolf Flesch, Ed. New York: Harper & Row, 1957.

Trelease, Jim. *The Read-Aloud Handbook.* New York: Viking Penguin Inc., 1985.

Vail, Priscilla Dr. *Smart Kids with School Problems.* New York: E.P. Dutton, 1987.

Webster's New World Dictionary of the American Language. New York: Warner Books, 1984.

What Works: Research About Teaching and Learning. United States Department of Education. William J. Bennett, Secretary, 1986.

Zimmerman, William. *Instant Oral Biographies.* New York: Guarionex Press, Ltd., 201 West 77th Street, New York, NY 10024, 1982.

Cheri Fuller, born in Dallas, Texas, was the fourth of six children. Home was a place where something interesting was always happening. Even as a small child, she remembers the art time, nature walks, backyard games, and playing school at home with her sisters. Because of these experiences, she learned to read before starting school. In the course of family life, she also began writing — long letters to grandparents and to an uncle who lived in Alaska, poems for birthday cards, and verses for special occasions.

Cheri has had extensive experience in teaching English and creative writing. She taught freshman composition at the university level, an inner city catch-up program for disadvantaged youth, public junior high, private college preparatory school, Christian elementary, junior high, and high school.

She also taught history and world geography. She has privately tutored, teamtaught, and written curriculum.

Through her teaching experience, she developed a concern for the sliding academic skills she saw in the classroom and wanted to use her experience to help parents provide an environment supportive to learning. This led her to research the causes and solutions to the school problems and to write a book for parents. She teaches workshops for parent groups and PTA's on topics such as learning style, encouraging reading and writing skills, and other topics, and teaches in the classroom young authors' workshops to encourage their writing skills.

Cheri holds a bachelor's degree in English, history, and secondary education, and a Master's degree in English Literature from Baylor University in Waco, Texas. She and her husband Holmes have three children: Justin, Chris and Alison.

To contact Cheri Fuller,
write:
Cheri Fuller
P. O. Box 770493
Oklahoma City, Oklahoma 73177

BOOKS FOR FAMILY LIFE

___ *STEPMOTHERING: ANOTHER KIND OF LOVE*
   Pearl Ketover Prilik 0-425-12050-3/$4.50
Stepfamily relationships are growing more common—yet the experience can still be a difficult one. This personal, positive approach offers intelligent and sensitive answers to a stepmother's everyday problems.

___ *GROWING UP HAPPY* by Bob Keeshan
   0-425-12315-4/$4.95
He brightened the mornings of three generations of children as TV's Captain Kangaroo. Now, this award winning performer offers heartwarming and practical advice on raising well-adjusted, happy children as he shares his thoughts on a wide range of topics—from the importance of your child's self-esteem to the challenges of parenting today.

___ *FOODS FOR HEALTHY KIDS* by Dr. Lendon Smith
   0-425-09276-3/$3.95
Dr. Lendon Smith, America's leading authority on nutrition for children, tells how to prevent and alleviate health problems such as asthma allergies, depression, constipation, hyperactivity, sleep problems and tension—not with medicine, but with good, nourishing food. He gives you his total nutrition program, complete with more than 100 recipes.

___ *LEARNINGAMES FOR THE FIRST THREE YEARS*
   Joseph Sparling & Isabelle Lewis 0-425-08847-2/$4.50
This book includes 100 fully-illustrated easy and fun adult-child games. All are designed to combine loving, playing and learning in an effective program that will enrich your child's life.

For Visa, MasterCard and American Express orders ($10 minimum) call: 1-800-631-8571

FOR MAIL ORDERS: CHECK BOOK(S). FILL OUT COUPON. SEND TO:	**POSTAGE AND HANDLING:** $1.50 for one book, 50¢ for each additional. Do not exceed $4.50.
BERKLEY PUBLISHING GROUP 390 Murray Hill Pkwy., Dept. B East Rutherford, NJ 07073	**BOOK TOTAL** $ _____
NAME_____	**POSTAGE & HANDLING** $ _____
ADDRESS_____	**APPLICABLE SALES TAX** $ _____ (CA, NJ, NY, PA)
CITY_____	**TOTAL AMOUNT DUE** $ _____
STATE_____ZIP_____	**PAYABLE IN US FUNDS.** (No cash orders accepted.)
PLEASE ALLOW 6 WEEKS FOR DELIVERY. PRICES ARE SUBJECT TO CHANGE WITHOUT NOTICE.	

THE BERKLEY TOTAL HEALTH SERIES:

THE PRACTICAL HOME HEALTH LIBRARY

__HIGH TIMES/LOW TIMES: How To Cope With Teenage Depression By John E. Meeks, M.D.** 0-425-11904-1/$3.95
Answers to the most commonly asked questions about coping with the most trying years of your child's development: the teenage years.

__LIGHT UP YOUR BLUES: A Guide To Overcoming Seasonal Depression and Fatigue By Robert N. Moreines, M.D.** 0-425-11782-0/$3.95
There is a cure for the wintertime blues! This is the definitive guide to identifying symptoms, understanding causes, and finding help with Seasonal Affective Disorder.

__NEW MEDICINES OF THE MIND: A Unique Consumer Guide To Today's Prescription Drugs By Irl Extein, M.D., Ph.D., Peter L. Herridge, M.D., Larry S. Kirstein, M.D.** 0-425-11879-7/$3.95
Learn the ABCs of today's "wonder drugs" and ensure the safe, effective, practical, and non-addictive use of the mood-stabilizing drugs your doctor prescribes.

__COMMON AND UNCOMMON SCHOOL PROBLEMS: A Parent's Guide By David A. Gross, M.D. and Irl L. Extein, M.D.** 0-425-12051-1/$3.95
A guide to help every concerned parent understand the normal stages that children go through, and how proper diagnosis and intervention can prevent serious school problems.

For Visa , MasterCard and American Express orders ($10 minimum) call: 1-800-631-8571

FOR MAIL ORDERS: CHECK BOOK(S). FILL OUT COUPON. SEND TO:

BERKLEY PUBLISHING GROUP
390 Murray Hill Pkwy., Dept. B
East Rutherford, NJ 07073

NAME_____

ADDRESS_____

CITY_____

STATE_____ZIP_____

PLEASE ALLOW 6 WEEKS FOR DELIVERY.
PRICES ARE SUBJECT TO CHANGE WITHOUT NOTICE.

POSTAGE AND HANDLING:
$1.50 for one book, 50¢ for each additional. Do not exceed $4.50.

BOOK TOTAL	$ _____
POSTAGE & HANDLING	$ _____
APPLICABLE SALES TAX (CA, NJ, NY, PA)	$ _____
TOTAL AMOUNT DUE	$ _____

PAYABLE IN US FUNDS.
(No cash orders accepted.)

272